👍 **Likes**

for CREATIVITY, SPIRITUALITY & MAKING A BUCK

"So many books about spirituality lack an acknowledgment of the day-to-day world, while most books about success lack an ethical and spiritual compass. David Nichtern figured out how to harmonize two essential modern human agendas. With humor and compassion for people who are uncomfortable with spiritual language, with impeccable logic and an open heart, David Nichtern explains how to intertwine spiritual and ethical principles with the pragmatic issues of day-to-day life.

"I first knew David Nichtern as a great guitar player and record producer. Then it turned out he was a big-deal teacher of Buddhism and now he has written this irresistible book. I'll have whatever he's having."—Danny Goldberg, former president of Atlantic Records, manager of Nirvana, and author of *In Search of the Lost Chord.*

"As much as David loves helping people connect to their Buddha nature, he loves helping young creatives turn their passions into their careers just as much. In this wonderful book, he gives away secrets most of us professional-artist types keep to ourselves. Lucky for you, his heart is big enough to share with everyone."—Pete Holmes, author of *Comedy Sex God*

"David Nichtern wonderfully shares the fruit of a long career and a wide variety of life experiences, along with his devoted meditation practice and exploration. Sound, tested, business planning and advice would seem to be an odd pairing with Buddhist teaching and guidance on how to establish a meditation practice. But *Creativity, Spirituality, and Making a Buck* proves this not to be the case. Tools like Tibetan *lojong* slogans, pithy bits of Buddhist wisdom teachings, can totally change your day."—Sharon Salzberg, author of *Real Happiness* and *Real Love*

"Growing up, I always worried that in order to be spiritual one needed the rules to live a simple, quiet life. As I gained a self and success I realized that none of us live simple lives. We ALL need help to understand that a modern life demands flexibility and freedom. David's new book gives us guidance and the tools to do so but mostly permission to be ambitious *and* still."—Jamie Lee Curtis

"Could you use a nudge to boost your creativity, income, or even your spiritual life? David Nichtern makes the perfect noodge. In *Creativity, Spirituality, and Making a Buck* he offers, as promised, solid steps to boost your creative spirit, your spiritual impulses, and your income. And in a day when there are zero public funds for creativity, creatives can use this as a handbook for funding themselves. Best: Nichtern waxes engaging and clever, wise, and funny—making this a book anyone can not only benefit from but also enjoy reading."—Daniel Goleman, author of *Altered Traits: How Meditation Transforms Your Mind, Brain, and Body*

"This is a wonderful book! If I were to create a workbook, this is what it would look like—it's so simple yet so effective. I highly recommend it!"—Anita Morrjani, author of the *New York Times* bestseller *Dying to Be Me*

"David is a master at helping us untangle the neurotic knots that often can get in the way of the creative process. This book will help you shake off some of the weird, superstitious bullshit you might be attaching to your dreams and give you some down-to-earth practices that can help ground your art and spirituality in a stable framework based on Buddhist principles.

"If, like me, you've attached a menagerie of irrational ideas and inefficient methods to your creative process, then this book could help you find a more stable, efficient, and powerful way to bring your ideas into the world."—Duncan Trussell, comedian and host of the *Duncan Trussell Family Hour* podcast

"This is a wonderful book that David may be uniquely qualified to write. For those of us who always wanted to live a creative or entrepreneurial life while also pursuing a mindful or spiritual practice, we often end up feeling like sellouts whenever we have to try to make an honest living. In the voice of a savvy and caring mentor, using a lifetime of wisdom from his three areas of expertise, a Buddhist teacher/musician/entrepreneur offers a personal and totally practical guide toward bringing your practice and your creative vision to the real world, where they can actually do some good. I plan to use his detailed exercises myself, and I recommend this book to anyone who is trying to wake up without leaving the modern world behind."—Ethan Nichtern, author of *The Road Home: A Contemporary Exploration of the Buddhist Path*

"'Making a buck' becomes a spiritual journey when we notice that our ordinary, daily life—job and all—is profoundly sacred. And there is no one more qualified to point this out than David Nichtern. With humor, wisdom, and creative grace, David helps us rediscover that livelihood can be a true, spiritual joy!"—Michael Carroll, author of *Awake at Work* and *The Mindful Leader*

"Buddhism and yoga recognize four aims of life: *dharma* (moral values, ethics), *artha* (economic values, money), *kama* (psychological values, enjoyment), and *moksha* (spiritual values, liberation). *Moksha* means release from the cycle of rebirth, and it is the final aim. But what do we do in the meantime? How do we live by ethical principles, create prosperity, enjoy creative fulfillment, and not jeopardize our chances for enlightenment?

"David Nichtern, a successful musician, businessman, and spiritual practitioner has devoted his life to the study of how the mind works and how the world works, and he hasn't neglected having a good time along the way. In his new book he shares his vast experience and wisdom in a practical, down-to-earth approach that will lift you out of humdrum reality into the wonderment of infinite possibilities."—Sharon Gannon, cofounder of the Jivamukti Yoga method

"Everybody has a hungry heart. We are hungry for so many different kinds of food. The table is set and the meal is laid out for us . . . but how do we put that food into our mouths and TASTE IT? In this book, David Nichtern guides us with wisdom, joy, and humor to make our whole lives a tasty meal to be enjoyed and shared with others."—Krishna Das, Grammy-nominated kirtan artist and author of *Chants of a Lifetime*

"A wonderful, practical guide to the balance between the spiritual life and capitalism. Mr. Nichtern exemplifies this union magnificently as both a renowned musician (performing with Krishna Das and many others), music-producer, and composer of scores for film and TV, as well as leading master meditation-teacher-training programs in Japan and the USA. Go order ASAP."—Master Sat Hon, founder of the New York Dan Tao Qigong School and author of *Taoist Qigong for Health and Vitality*

"Most people associate spirituality with an ethereal escape from everyday life, a way to separate from the world of work, bills, and money. David Nichtern, long-time Buddhist teacher, renowned musician, life coach, and one of my most esteemed go-to Buddhist advisors, teaches us that we can make money without giving up on our spiritual aspirations and live our spiritual aspirations without turning our backs on the material world."—Susan Piver, author of *The Four Noble Truths of Love*

"David Nichtern has created a masterpiece for us to learn from and enjoy. Weaving together his life experiences as musician, composer, deep Dharma seeker, and entrepreneur, he offers profound guidance for living a life aligned with inner purpose while thriving along the twists and turns as they unfold. With great humor and self-deprecation, David, like a favorite uncle, gives spiritual guidance and practical wisdom."—Stephan Rechtschaffen, founder of Omega Institute and Blue Spirit Retreat Center (Costa Rica)

"David has done it again! *Creativity, Spirituality, and Making a Buck* beautifully weaves together David's lifetime of accumulated knowledge as a world-renowned meditation teacher, successful entrepreneur, and celebrated musician. This book is both light and deep, a rare combination that makes reading a joy while prompting you to look inward. I highly recommend this book to anyone looking to explore the balance of spirituality and living in today's modern world."—Stephen Sokoler, founder and CEO of Journey Meditation

CREATIVITY
SPIRITUALITY
& MAKING A
BUCK

DAVID NICHTERN

Wisdom Publications
199 Elm Street
Somerville, MA 02144 USA
wisdompubs.org

Library of Congress Cataloging-in-Publication Data

Names: Nichtern, David, author.
Title: Creativity, spirituality & making a buck / David Nichtern.
Other titles: Creativity, spirituality, and making a buck
Description: Somerville, MA : Wisdom Publications, 2019.
Identifiers: LCCN 2019016594 (print) | ISBN 9781614294986 (pbk. : alk. paper)
Subjects: LCSH: Spiritual life. | Creative ability–Religious aspects. | Creation (Liter-
    ary, artistic, etc.)–Religious aspects. | Success in business–Religious aspects.
Classification: LCC BL624 .N524 2019 (print) | LCC BL624 (ebook) | DDC
    294.3/444–dc23
LC record available at https://lccn.loc.gov/2019016594
LC ebook record available at https://lccn.loc.gov/2019980906

ISBN 978-1-61429-498-6   ebook ISBN 978-1-61429-518-1

23 22 21 20 19
5 4 3 2 1

Cover design by David Henry Lantz. Interior design by Gopa & Ted2, Inc.
Set in ITC New Baskerville 10.5/15.

MIX
Paper from
responsible sources
FSC
www.fsc.org FSC® C005010

Please visit fscus.org.

For Chögyam Trungpa Rinpoche
and Izzy Atlas Nichtern

Contents

Preface

This book is intended to help you clarify your objectives in life and accomplish them.

Regardless of your specific circumstances, there are basic principles that apply to all aspects of living—these fundamentals can be helpful to learn, contemplate, and apply to your current reality. Some of the principles we're going to explore together are ancient, passed along through the human chain of existence; some are just good common sense; and some arise in the experiential process of engaging the world on its own terms.

An important part of the framework for this book is derived from Buddhist teachings; this is a natural outgrowth of the fact that I've studied, practiced, and taught in that tradition for forty-five years. But the essence of the book is, I believe, completely universal and should apply to all of us—no matter what our particular religious or philosophical background might be.

The approach taken here probably falls into the category of what Tibetans call "grandmother's advice": solid, experience-based support from a little old lady who has traveled some of these pathways and is, as we bujus (Buddhist Jews) would say, *kibitzing* (coaching from the bleachers) or *nudging* (minding the other person's business). In this case, the little old lady is me. This is how I earned my nickname, "nudgiebuju."

The advice has been organized into some guiding principles to help you access these timeless Buddhist teachings and make this *sechel* (worldly smarts) easier to access for ordinary folks like ourselves.

For most of my adult life, I've been teaching Buddhism and mentoring individual students, as well as leading a substantial double/triple life as a professional composer, guitarist, and producer, and as an entrepreneur. I've received four Emmys, two Grammy nominations, and several gold and platinum records; run several of my own businesses (including two record labels); and worked with people like Jerry Garcia, Stevie Wonder, Paul Simon, Christopher Guest, Maria Muldaur, Lana Del Rey, and Krishna Das. Grandma has been around.

Much of what I'm going to talk about herein was learned the hard way—through direct personal experience and paying lots of dues. Hopefully, if nothing else, you can learn from my many mistakes and possibly save yourself years, if not decades, of valuable time as you move toward crystallizing and manifesting your vision of your life here on earth.

I've found that success and failure are both valuable teachers. Having said that, I don't wish failure on anybody, unless you need to receive a message about humility, perfecting your craft or business skills further, or just generally softening and opening to the full experience of being alive, which clearly includes loss, disappointment, understanding impermanence, and the need to become more compassionate to oneself and others along the way.

When I say I wish success for people, I want to be clear that here we're not simply defining success as getting what you *thought* you wanted—or just manifesting a giant bank account. We each have to define success on our own terms, in as complete and unique a way as possible. If we choose to, we can include in this definition our personal well-being and the well-being of our family, community, society, and all sentient beings sharing this beautiful earth.

In any case, if you're trying to integrate your creativity, your overall sense of well-being (spiritual, emotional, psychological, and physical), and the challenges of managing your livelihood, I think this book could be helpful to you.

For some time now, I've been teaching workshops—based on this theme—at Dharma centers, yoga studios, holistic learning institutions, and online. I've seen bankers beatbox hip-hop with their mouths. I've seen teachers, creatives, and young entrepreneurs struggle with the basic principles of starting a business. And I've seen people struggle to wrap their minds around what meditation is and how to actually do it—and discover what, if anything, it might have to do with their everyday lives.

My online workshop for creativelive.com, which was also called "Creativity, Spirituality & Making A Buck," could be an interesting companion piece for this book: davidnichtern.com/csmb

Until recently, I separated the three topics of creativity, spirituality, and livelihood into three distinct segments in my workshops and trainings. It has been really intriguing to watch people's energy shift as they move from meditation to creativity to business. But in preparing to write this book, I decided to take a leap and begin to integrate these topics in order to explore the principles they might have in common.

I have an almost lifelong obsession with the classical and largely accepted divide between the spiritual and secular dimensions of life ("Render unto Caesar . . ."). My Buddhist teacher, Chögyam Trungpa Rinpoche (sometimes herein referred to as CTR), made a very big deal about integrating these seemingly disparate aspects of our lives. In my own way I'm following suit and mapping the principle of integration through the filter of my own experience and expression.

The very first Buddhist seminar I attended was in 1970 with CTR. It was somewhat surprisingly titled "Work, Sex, and Money." An astute observer will notice that, for the time being, I've held in reserve the topics of sexuality, romance, and relationships, which on their own are very deep and complex subjects and certainly a significant part of a life well lived. If you're interested in reading about relationships, there are so many great books, too numerous to mention here. But *this* book will explore fundamental principles related to three aspects of our lives—creativity, spirituality, and making a buck—and how they can intersect and cross-pollinate to create a full and rich existence.

My aspiration is that this book will help you make sense of your personal life-puzzle, that you'll walk away from this exploration inspired, emboldened, and grounded in real-life wisdom to define success the way you choose—and then achieve it.

Getting Started
How to Use This Book

THIS BOOK IS FOR YOU. Of course, you can simply read through it, noting any ideas that are relevant or possibly helpful to support you in your life's journey. But I've also included several other layers that might significantly enhance your capacity not just to appreciate the ideas expressed but also really connect with them personally—and begin to improve the quality of your life. Ultimately it's your own process of discovery and personal evolution that's the focus of this book.

ABOUT YOUR WORKBOOK

A major layer of this "interactive" book is the inclusion of a free downloadable workbook—available at wisdomexperience.org/creativity-online-workbook—for you to fill out as you go along, but you're also welcome to use whatever blank notebook you'd like. All the questions and writing prompts are included both in this book and in the downloadable workbook, so you can work in the medium that best fits your process. Each will be marked with this symbol, so they will be easy to find:

Sometimes the workbook will invite you to respond to questions that feel very familiar—maybe even obvious. But it could provide you with an opportunity to take a fresh look at your life and address basic issues that can sometimes get buried underneath the rubble of managing your day-to-day to-do lists.

ABOUT THE MANIFESTORS

In creative pursuits, spiritual practice, and business, it can be so helpful to draw on the wisdom of those who have modeled the qualities we seek to cultivate. These individuals can inspire us to clarify our own process, illuminate the way forward, and in ideal circumstances sometimes even offer personal guidance and mentoring.

There will be quotes from a variety of "manifestors" sprinkled throughout the book. Additionally, among the other supporting materials for the book, I've created an exclusive set of podcast-style interviews with an array of friends, colleagues, and "successful" (in various ways) individuals who have mastered some or all of the principles we're going to be exploring.

You will find a link to these podcasts at my website: davidnichtern.com/podcast

These interviews stand on their own but can also be a powerful adjunct to the flow of information in this book. You can access them as you connect with relevant material herein or at any time, at your own pace, for your enjoyment and further edification.

ABOUT THE BUDDHIST INFLUENCE IN THIS BOOK: *AS IT IS* AND *UP TO YOU*

As I mentioned, there will be a thread of Buddhist teachings throughout this book. The Dharma (Buddha's teachings) has intellectual depth and subtlety, but it's also loaded with practical advice that's accessible and can be immediately useful. My intention is to unpack these teachings in a way that is grounded, authentic, and genuinely productive in our everyday worldly existence. That practical thread is an important element in how the Buddha taught and how my own Buddhist teacher, Chögyam Trungpa Rinpoche, taught.

Also, any expression of rigid dogma will be unintentional. A principal part of the Buddhist tradition is to invite the student to carefully examine the teachings and verify them through personal evaluation. Everything is offered in the spirit of "for your consideration." So in this presentation, please feel free to take the best and leave the rest.

There's a Sanskrit word in Buddhism, *tathata*, that means "as it is." Not as you wish it was, not as you think it is, not as it appears to be, but *as it is*. There are certain underlying principles and realities in our world that are simply *as it is*. We don't get to vote on *as it is*. Gravity could be one example of such a principle; we don't get to vote on whether or not gravity exists. Try jumping up and not coming down if you don't believe me.

However, we do get to vote on how we're going to *relate* to *as it is*. At the same time we discover *as it is*, we can explore another Buddhist premise, which we're going to call *up to us*. For example, try doing twenty-five jumping jacks right now to increase your cardiovascular health. In that case, the gravity would be *as it is* but using it to your advantage would be *up to you*! How we see ourselves, what we aspire to in life, what we achieve—all of it is *up to us*.

These are two core principles in this book: *as it is* and *up to us*. We'll be exploring these principles further.

ABOUT PRACTICE ALERTS

Throughout the book I've also included a series of "practice alerts"; these will be signaled by this symbol:

When you see this marking, you'll be invited to put your book down for a while and work directly with your own mind and body in a variety of ways. The essence of practice is to allow some time to examine your own experience directly.

There will be meditation techniques, contemplation practices, and various cultivations intended to help you mix your mind with the ideas we're exploring together.

You can follow the directions, extend the time indicated, or simply skip over these sections (it's up to you!), and continue your reading if you prefer. You can also return to the practices described anytime, at your own pace and in your own way.

Actually, the twenty-five jumping jacks we just did was a sneaky practice alert—but don't worry, most of them will be more contemplative!

ABOUT THE LINKS

Throughout the book I'll be placing all kinds of URLs to other sources—books, articles, recordings, and videos—that might enhance the experience of taking this ride with me.

These days, I've found myself wishing that every dinner party or gathering I go to could have one additional guest: Siri! If you've found yourself in a lively conversation recently and wanting to share an article, a book, a song, or a movie as part of the thread, to wander through and return, to ramble, regress, digress, look ahead, and then continue, these links will be fun for you. Some might be shameless plugs!

If not, if you're more linear and less random-access than me and some of the rest of us, you can just bypass these links. They will, in a sense, replace the concept of footnotes and additional references at the end of the book. You can meander through them and come back to your reading when you're finished, or you can just note these links and return to them whenever you're in the mood. If you're reading in digital format, many of these will be a simple click away; otherwise copying and pasting next time you're online should do the trick. They will be formatted like this, so they'll be easy to find:

All the links will be hosted on my website so that I can edit them when necessary or add to them when I discover great new content that I want to share with you. So check the page out and see what you think: davidnichtern.com/links

ABOUT THE SLOGANS

Finally, also sprinkled throughout the text you'll find short, pithy, one- or two-line slogans. If you're like me, sometimes attempting to absorb acres of more subtle narrative can be facilitated by getting directly to the essential point. Sometimes that's all I remember anyhow.

In Buddhism, very short and incisive comments by the teacher are sometimes called *pith instructions*. They cut right to the heart of the matter, and you usually remember them and chew on them for years—or even decades.

Dilgo Khyentse Rinpoche, my teacher's teacher, one of the Dalai Lama's teachers, and generally acknowledged as one of the greatest Tibetan Buddhist masters of the twentieth century, once pulled aside a senior teacher in our community for a pith instruction. After much ado to set up the right situation, he whispered in his ear, "Be kind to everyone."

That was it. You figure out how to do it. I'm still working on it.

Krishna Das, kirtan (chanting) maestro and my amigo—I've produced several of his records and play guitar with him on tour whenever I'm able—tells many such stories about his Indian guru, Neem

Karoli Baba. He was known throughout his community as Maharaji, which literally means "great king," even though as far as I can tell he only appeared to own two things: a cotton robe and a blanket. Even those things he would give away periodically—interesting notion of royalty, no?

Maharaji was famously introduced to Westerners through the books of Ram Dass (Richard Alpert), author of *Be Here Now*, who often quotes Maharaji as saying "Love everyone and tell the truth."

Maybe this sounds like a Hallmark greeting card, maybe it sounds obvious, maybe it sounds impossible, but I've *often* contemplated that deceptively simple direction. It's a great calibration for setting our ethical compasses.

Such comments from great masters can live on as lofty and profound pith instructions. There might be one or two attempts at such eternal wisdom herein, but really this book is filled more with every-day, garden-variety nuggets that aim to help you know the terrain in which you're operating, make a clear assessment of the situation, and move forward incisively and skillfully.

Here are a few examples to illustrate the flavor of these slogans:

> With meditation practice there are various benefits, but none of them can be realized if you don't **make the time to actually practice.**

> The need to create may be a personal one—but for your creation to serve a market or an audience, you must **be aware of the needs of others.**

> If your time and energy are spread too thinly across a variety of (possibly wonderful) offerings, some or all of them may falter.

Good leaders take responsibility. If you find that you're constantly pointing out the shortcomings of others, turn the mirror around so it's facing you.

Take your mind to the gym. Just as you can train your body to develop strength, flexibility, and stamina, you can also train your mind to develop clarity, focus, and stability.

So keep an eye out for these. Some of these are derived from my previous workshops. Others are brand-new. A few are traditional Buddhist slogans, some of which are derived from a style of teaching called *lojong*, or "mind training." In lojong practice we read, memorize, and then contemplate and reflect on a specific group of simple but pithy slogans as they arise in everyday life situations. These traditional Buddhist slogans will be marked with this:

They will all be included in appendix 2 of this book, so if you can't remember anything else you read, just copy that page—or if you're reading the ebook, cut and paste it—and, when you get on the subway next Thursday morning, pick a slogan to contemplate in the field as you watch your world swirl around you!

Ready? Let's begin.

Let's make our first visit to your workbook. When you finish your entry, come back, and we'll continue on to the next chapter.

1. "How're You Doin'?"

I would like to invite you to take a moment to write a short assessment of your major aspirations in life and your current appraisal of how you're moving toward realizing those aspirations.

Be spontaneous and just express yourself honestly. Former mayor of New York City Ed Koch used to walk through the streets of the city asking random passersby, "How'm I doin'?" So now I'm inviting you to start your process by asking you, "How're you doin'?" Toward the end of our project I'll invite you to update your answer.

Just take a shot for now, in your workbook, at answering this simple yet revealing question. People ask us this question frequently. If they only really knew!

Here you can be completely straightforward and as thorough as you wish to be. Remember—nobody ever has to see your workbook besides you, unless you choose to share it! And there's no good reason to lie to yourself. In this workbook, you don't have to worry about impressing anybody or receiving uncomfortable feedback and unreasonable expectations. You don't even have to edit or critique yourself. Just take those grouchy old Muppets in the balcony and eject them from the theater right now!

So, "How're you doin'?"

Part **I** Basic Principles:
The OS for Enlightened Living

IN PART 1 we're going to lay some groundwork for our project of integrating creativity, spirituality, and making a buck. We'll be talking about some basic principles that are pervasive and foundational.

When I teach these days, I like to say that we're learning principles, not rules. Rules only apply in a system where the situation remains static, which is rarely the case in real life.

Principles, however, can be adapted to changing situations, even though the principles themselves remain constant. Gravity, for example, is a principle, not a rule. If you're on a spaceship, gravity is still present, but it might behave differently. If you understand the *principle* of gravity, you can adapt it to the feeling of weightlessness you might experience in outer space.

The underlying principle of this book is that it's possible to move toward balance, prosperity, happiness, and basic sanity in our lives as human beings. The core of the operating system that will get us there is recognizing how our minds work and how the world works—deepening our understanding of ourselves and the world in which we live.

Integral to that kind of knowledge is developing a clear vision of where we've been, where we are, and where we're going; and how clarity, intention, and effort can help bring about a more beneficial outcome for ourselves and others.

1 Joining Heaven and Earth

Spiritual and mystical suggest something rarefied, otherworldly, and loftily religious, opposed to an ordinary material life which is simply practical and commonplace. The whole point . . . is to show the fallacy of this opposition, to show that the spiritual is not to be separated from the material, nor the wonderful from the ordinary.

—ALAN WATTS, *This Is It: And Other Essays on Zen and Spiritual Experience*

IN THIS BOOK, we're exploring the process of creating a vision for our lives and making it happen. There are many ways to talk about manifesting our vision, but one classic form is the notion of "joining heaven and earth."

In many Asian cultures, some European cultures, and the Shambhala teachings I studied, joining heaven and earth is presented as the responsibility of leadership in particular, and of human beings in general.

Heaven represents opening our minds, expanding our horizons, and envisioning possibilities. Earth represents being practical, grounded, and mastering all the tiny details of life. When heaven and earth are joined, or synchronized, we can experience harmony and prosperity.

If we look through the lens of heaven and earth, we can often see when and how our grand schemes go off the trail and into the weeds. Sometimes we have big visions, big plans, and all our moves are lined up and ready to go. Then suddenly, seemingly out of nowhere, we don't have the right circumstances, the right help, the right resources, the right amount of money, the right weather—you name it.

Our heaven, or vision, was so clear, so good, so right, but we've literally and figuratively run aground. We've crashed into earth, and suddenly our lofty dream turns into a challenging one, maybe even a nightmare. In these cases, we may temporarily connect with the heaven principle but we lose our connection with the earth.

However, sometimes we're so efficient, so capable, so much in control of the details of our life—but something is missing. The whole enterprise starts to feel hollow and meaningless. In this case, we don't seem to have a clear vision; there's no big picture—we're simply operating to get our ever-growing to-do list accomplished. But what's it all for? What's the meaning? In this case, we've conquered earth but lost heaven.

When I teach Buddhism in Japan these days (which is so frequently that some of my friends think I live there), I often stay in a hotel that on a clear day has a view of Mount Fuji. Even though the mountain is more than fifty miles away, with its snow-capped peak it seems to penetrate and sometimes even dominate the surrounding and intense imagery of a wildly urbanized Tokyo.

I like to see Mount Fuji because it reminds me of the vast and unobstructed sense of "heaven," of the open and clear quality of the Buddha's teachings and the reset button we can always push to allow ourselves a more spacious and open state of mind. It's helpful to periodically connect with the heaven principle—however we can access it.

Whether we're aware of it or not, we each already have some kind of vision for our life. Maybe it's modest: just getting by, having a little comfort—a reasonable life. From there our vision could expand to include becoming a great artist, musician, architect, meditation teacher, parent, benefactor, healer, president—you name it. In the realm of heaven, the sky is literally the limit.

This vision can involve our whole life—relationships, family, children, creative outlets, money, lifestyle, etc. Some people might say they're just going with the flow—why do we have to be so *deliberate* about our process? I myself probably lean in this direction more than some.

However, if we really examine our life, I think we can say that there's some underlying vision, whether it's explicit or not. Even "going with the flow" can be a kind of vision statement.

When we explore the making-a-buck part of our lives, the notion of joining heaven and earth can be a very useful construct and an extremely practical approach.

Contemplating our vision can help us connect more directly with the actual journey we're undertaking. Regarding our work life, we might think we're clear as a bell and right on target, or we might be feeling lost, double-crossed, and forgotten—or anything in between.

As we descend from our lofty view of Mount Fuji, our vast sense of possibilities and opportunities, let's see if we can apply this notion of heaven and earth to our own livelihood and career.

2. Joining Heaven and Earth

Please take a shot at briefly and succinctly answering the following questions.

It can sometimes be helpful to allow your "first thought," as CTR used to say, to come through spontaneously when answering these questions, and then contemplate for a while and take a second pass at answering. At the end of this entire process, your workbook will become a self-portrait—and perhaps an important tool in bringing your heaven and earth into alignment.

Livelihood Heaven Questionnaire

1. Describe your vision for your professional life. What would be your ideal job or career?

2. Define your current livelihood. What do you *do* at work?

3. Would you rather be doing something else? If so, what?

4. How much money do you make? How much would you like to make?

5. Write down any other thoughts or considerations you want to include.

Livelihood Earth Questionnaire

1. What skills do you need to create the career you're visualizing?

2. Do you need more training to be fully prepared for the job you really want?

3. Do you live in the right place to do the job you really want? (For example, do you live in Kansas and want to be an oceanographer?)

4. Do you have sufficient liquid assets (cash)?

5. Do you have the right *support team*? Accountant? Bookkeeper, lawyer, social media wizard, administrative assistant? A good mentor(s) as you move into areas that may be less familiar to you?

6. Write down any other thoughts or considerations you want to include.

2 Cultivating Mindfulness

Clarity, Intention, and Effort

One of the greatest lessons that comes from meditation is that a relaxed curiosity about life and sleepwalking through it are two radically different choices.

—ETHAN NICHTERN, *One City: A Declaration of Interdependence*

If your mind is a runaway train, your life will be a runaway life.

WHEN I'M WORKING one-on-one mentoring individual students, we base our training, in substantial part, on developing a regular meditation practice. This is a wonderful way to cultivate a grounded and clear state of mind. And in my opinion, when combined with ethics, mindfulness meditation makes a great foundation for leading a life worth living.

Once the foundation of mindfulness and ethical conduct is established as the backbone of our spiritual well-being—and enshrined in a routine we call *practice*—we begin to expand outward to explore our everyday life as a mirror and measure of our practice. How is our work going? Creative outlets? Relationships?

In order to join heaven and earth, in order to create harmony, whether in livelihood or other areas of our lives, we're going to need *clarity*, *intention*, and *effort*.

CLARITY

In the last several years, mindfulness meditation, which has been around for at least twenty-five hundred years, has become somewhat of a hit (as we would say in the record business). It has been plucked from the much more expansive body of Buddhist teachings and put into heavy rotation as support for regular folks like us to develop focus, balance, and peace of mind.

Meanwhile, contemporary neuroscientists have joined the chorus of mindfulness proponents, with various reproducible test results demonstrating positive influences on the brain of the meditator—adding intensity to the wider interest in meditation.

The popularity of mindfulness is a good thing. In Japan, magazines are suddenly all talking about the "mindfulness movement." Even banks and other corporations, in the West *and* in Asia, seem to want a piece of this action. Companies like Google, Nike, Morgan Stanley, Viacom, Sony, Facebook, and Disney all have some version of mindfulness meditation programs in place—many through a company I work with called Journey Meditation. Recently a company I also work with, True Nature Meditation, in Japan, started a mindfulness program at Goldman Sachs in Tokyo, as part of a larger "resilience" program they initiated to support the well-being of their employees. Several major sport franchises, including the Super Bowl–winning Seattle Seahawks, have featured mindfulness programs as well.

I personally find this development reasonable and predictable in the West but somewhat astonishing in Japan, since Buddhism was introduced there some fifteen hundred years ago. It's possible there are more Buddha statues per square foot in Japan than anywhere else on earth—more Buddhas than Starbucks! Many people there would call themselves Buddhist but don't associate that identity with some kind of regular meditation practice; in fact, many modern Japanese people seem to associate actual meditation with an obsolete religiosity. Many of them see mindfulness as a new trend!

However, if mindfulness is a trend or a fad, then it would be accurate to say that it's a twenty-five-hundred-year-old fad. It has "trended" many times during that period, in many cultures, places, and times.

In any case, whether we come to the practice through tradition or science, I'm taking the liberty here of suggesting that mindfulness meditation can be a wonderful foundation for us to clarify our vision, manifest that vision, and have a great life. I am prescribing it!

The only caveat is that we recognize that mindfulness isn't a magic pill or a weekend workshop we take once and then we're done. Meditation is a lifelong cultivation of our most basic assets and skills as human beings—our ability to be present and awake to our situation; to our mind, emotions, sense perceptions, circumstances, family, community, society, and the natural world around us.

Often the main thing blocking our ability to be present and see clearly is that our minds are too busy and too unstable. The Tibetan word *kuntag* refers to an illusory sense of reality, an overlay of projections and filters we project onto things as they are. CTR translated it as "random fixation." Our untrained minds are used to jumping from topic to topic, obsessing for a brief moment on whatever arises and then jumping like a frog to the next topic. So sometimes we call this kind of mind "frog mind" or "monkey mind"—or "spaghetti mind" (for foodies) or "James Joyce mind" (for the literati).

It usually takes less than a minute of mindfulness meditation to notice this random busyness of our mental activity. Many people who attempt to meditate start with the notion that their job is to silence this everyday mind, which is extremely difficult to do and not really the point anyway.

That approach can lead to a kind of tightness, self-aggression, and often a sense of failure, or, on the other hand, a kind of dull trance-like state without real awareness—kind of the spiritual equivalent to taking a tranquilizer.

Instead of trying to fight our mind, when we practice mindfulness, we simply bring our attention back to our breath over and over again. This is the key to settling our mind. Our mind is like the surface of a lake: when the wind settles down, the lake becomes clear and reflective.

In mindfulness meditation, we stabilize our mind by focusing our attention on a singular stimulus, such as paying attention to the feeling and texture of our breathing. This aspect of the practice is called *shamatha* in Sanskrit and has been translated as "one-pointed concentration" or "calm abiding." It's like being on a boat and recognizing that we're in rocky waters, so we drop an anchor—a singular point of steadiness to stabilize our motion. When we do notice our thoughts and emotions rocking and rolling, we simply return our attention to our breathing.

The second aspect of our mindfulness meditation practice is called *vipashyana* in Sanskrit and can be understood as awareness, insight, or clarity. We simply observe what arises in our mind without judgment or manipulation.

Vipashyana also allows us to see that there is space between and around our thoughts and that they are not actually as substantial and solid as we make them out to be.

What's most commonly described as "mindfulness meditation" in the current vernacular actually often has these two elements combined. Shamatha (stability) allows our mind to settle somewhat and vipashyana (clear-seeing) allows us to see our everyday mind exactly as it is, impartially, with gentleness and precision.

In our everyday lives, whenever we feel lost or confused regarding our big vision or current reality, practicing mindfulness meditation can be like hitting a reset button. You power down, let your engine (your mind) cool down for a few minutes, and then restart. This practice can help us restore our energy and regain perspective and balance.

Mindfulness meditation is highly recommended for clarifying our heaven and navigating our earth. Many times, even our making-a-buck issues are related to not having developed enough stability or clarity of mind—our business or creative problems are actually spiritual problems in disguise.

I know that it might be more popular to separate out the theory and result of mindfulness from the actual practice, but I can't do it in good conscience. You have to actually *practice* to achieve these scientifically verifiable results!

> With meditation practice there are various benefits,
> but none of them can be realized if you don't
> **make the time to actually practice.**

Mindfulness of Breath

Here's a simple mindfulness meditation practice you can do anytime, anywhere, for any length of time. Even if you're an experienced meditator, it can be very powerful to simply come back to this practice.

I would like to recommend that you put your book down right now for five minutes, take a good seated position, and actually *do* this mindfulness practice. For those of you not familiar with mindfulness meditation, a more in-depth instruction is in appendix 1. But for now, to keep it simple, here's how to do this practice in three easy steps:

1. Take a good upright posture ("upright but not uptight," as we meditation teachers sometimes say), either cross-legged on the floor, kneeling, or sitting on a chair. Try leaving your eyes slightly open, with a soft downward gaze resting about six feet on the floor in front of you. This will allow you to

include your sense perceptions and sensations as part of the larger environment of your meditation rather than trying to cut them off and go into some kind of inner trancelike state.

2. Place your attention on your breath going in and out of your body. Try to be fully present while paying attention to your breath and being open to whatever arises in your mind without clinging, manipulating, or trying to repress it.

3. When you notice you're lost in thought, you can simply say the word *thinking* (quietly to yourself) and bring your attention gently back to your breath as your primary focal point.

OK . . . so let's practice for five minutes.

Great job? Terrible job? Whatever happens in your practice is OK. Just practicing as above is the main point. Don't get lost in trying to achieve specific results. When you notice your mind has wandered, just come back. That's your practice.

Here's a video called "Taking Your Seat: Simple Meditation Instructions for Ordinary People," which has further instructions for mindfulness practice: davidnichtern.com/meditation

Take your mind to the gym. Just as you can train your body to develop strength, flexibility, and stamina, you can also train your mind to develop clarity, focus, and stability.

INTENTION

In our mindfulness practice we begin to more clearly see the ramblings of our monkey mind. One thing we may also notice as our practice progresses, in addition to this very active and somewhat random quality, is that we have very strongly ingrained habits—narratives that are deeply etched and often repeated.

We tend to create familiar territory by recycling certain thoughts and emotions that support our current conceptions of who we think we are. As we would say about a radio, video, or online hit—these thoughts are in heavy rotation in the media of our mind. If we practice meditation, we can activate the impartial observer I mentioned above and see these patterns clearly, from a newly disengaged, more objective point of view.

It's more challenging, however, to change the most deeply etched patterns of thoughts, either by simply letting them go or shifting to a different narrative. Mental habits are similar to physical habits such as laziness, bad posture, nervous tics, etc. Mental habits can become embedded—like plaque that gathers on our teeth and won't come off with a casual brushing.

So the first step is to cultivate the clarity to see the shape of our habits, which is a tremendous accomplishment in itself—it's kind of like a fish seeing the water in which it's swimming. Then, having made inroads into this kind of clear-seeing, the next step is to shift our habits.

In some sense, seeing and shifting our habitual patterns is the essence of spiritual practice and genuine success in life. Otherwise, no matter how externally successful we may appear to be, we're still stuck in a rigid and lifeless inner world—without real subtlety, dynamic movement, and insight.

In order to change, we first need to create a clear intention to do so. Otherwise the force and inertia of our habitual mind will reassert itself over and over again. It's like dieting—without a genuine intention to lose weight, we'll simply make superficial efforts, succeed for a while perhaps, and then go right back to where we were.

Let's go to your workbook.

3. Identifying and Releasing Our Habits

1. Identify three deeply ingrained habits that you can recognize as redundant, counterproductive obstacles to your personal growth and evolution.

2. Identify the narrative that accompanies the experience of those habitual patterns. For example: "I am often resentful—I feel disregarded and I deserve greater recognition for my talent, skill, and fabulous personality."

3. Identify any emotional flavors (such as anger, craving, disappointment, despair) that accompany the experience of those patterns.

4. Identify any physical sensations that accompany the experience of those patterns.

5. Describe what it feels like when you attempt to let go of those patterns—for example, by simply releasing the narrative and feelings as you become aware of them. Panic? Anxiety? Fear? Relief? Spaciousness? Humor?

EFFORT

Now let's bring this whole discussion of joining heaven and earth down to earth. How can we use this concept in a very practical and grounded way in our business life? Our making-a-buck life? Let's start there.

Joining our vision and our practicality to our livelihood will take *effort*. We have to exert ourselves. The law of inertia says that if we're stuck, we'll tend to remain stuck; and if we're moving in the wrong direction, we'll tend to keep moving in that direction.

One of the obstacles to exertion is, of course, laziness. In order to rouse ourselves, take a fresh look, create a vision for our livelihood, create strong intention to follow through on our vision, and face the myriad practical challenges and difficulties that will arise along the way, we'll need to overcome our laziness.

There are (at least) two kinds of laziness. The first and most familiar is a kind of lethargy or heaviness in which we simply can't get our engine going. We're too lazy to examine our situation, too lazy to practice mindfulness and awareness, too lazy to even see—let alone begin to change—our habitual patterns. The constant companion of this kind of laziness is, of course, procrastination.

The second kind of laziness is perhaps less obvious. We're too busy, too speedy, too obsessed with knocking off our to-do list to leave any space for developing clarity and intention. We're continually generating distractions and our busyness seems to feed on itself, like a snake eating its own tail. It's interesting to think of this kind of obsessive activity as a form of laziness, isn't it?

Let's go to your workbook.

4. Identifying Obstacles

1. Do you feel that you have a clear vision for your livelihood? If so, write it down concisely.

2. If not, please take five minutes (or a series of five-minute sessions) and contemplate your vision. Then write it down.

   Remember that vision isn't a tactical statement. You're not yet ready to develop a strategy for accomplishing your vision, let alone a tactical plan to execute that strategy. You're in the realm of pure vision now. Just express or update your aspiration for your livelihood, right here.

3. Now let's look at the obstacles that come up for you in moving forward with creating your livelihood vision on the ground, here on earth, in real time. Can you identify your most commonly experienced obstacles? Fear, doubt, paranoia,

self-hatred, impatience, arrogance, time, money, family dramas, support, clarity?

4. Can you identify your style of laziness? How do resistance, lethargy, and too much distraction play into your ability to clarify your vision, sharpen your intention, and begin to execute your livelihood aspiration?

One last note about effort: Try to keep a light touch and enjoy the process, rather than taking a heavy-handed and humorless approach. Here's the advice given by Doutreval of Dijon in the film *Scaramouche*: "A sword is like a bird. If you clutch it too tightly, you choke it—too lightly and it flies away."

3 Success and Contentment

Certainly in the West, there's a thing—bigger is better. I started to get into that when we were looking at doing multiple Omegas and multiple conferences. But the Small Is Beautiful movement has a lot to say also.

—STEPHAN RECHTSHAFFEN, founder of Omega Institute (New York) and Blue Spirit Retreat Center (Costa Rica)

SUCCESS

WHEN WE ATTEMPT to clarify and manifest our vision, we're setting up a framework for success or failure.

Many of us have imported our notion of success from our family, our community, our teachers, our heroes, our churches, or our society. When it comes to our vision—our heaven—we might be trying to become the richest person on the planet, the most famous, the most powerful, the most beautiful, the most brilliant, the happiest, the most compassionate, the most enlightened. From a materialistic point of view, we might have certain standards, gauging how successful we are by how much money we're making, what kind of clothes we wear, what kind of house we live in, what kind of car we drive.

Even in the spiritual world, there are still benchmarks of how "realized" or "enlightened" we are, how compassionate, how wise, how generous, how accomplished in studies and practices. We'll absolutely find these kinds of standards of success in spiritual communities. In a sense, they might be inverted from worldly standards—perhaps they're based on the absence of materialistic values, for instance—but they're similar in the sense that they imply what we currently have isn't sufficient or adequate. Success is somehow still off in the future.

What's missing from both arenas is a sense of contentment and satisfaction.

So how do we define success and contentment? How can we create a healthy sense of aspiration without dwelling on our shortcomings and setting ourselves up for ongoing failure and disappointment?

Whatever our sense of aspiration is, whatever our notion of success is—spiritual and temporal—we should formulate it on our own terms, having contemplated, processed, and digested appropriate input, feedback, and impressions. We can and should develop the strength and independence to set our own goals and set sail toward achieving them.

Whether we realize it or not, we probably already have some notion of what it means to be successful—and in all likelihood it's some combination of worldly benefits and spiritual values.

Let's go to your workbook.

5. Defining Success

1. Define your overall notion of success. What would it mean for you to be a successful person?
2. What does worldly success mean to you? Define worldly success in terms of income and other benefits: possessions, living situation, relationships, etc. At what point would you say, "I have all the things I want; I am content; I am satisfied"?

3. Now define spiritual success in your own terms. What qualities would you like to cultivate? Would you like to be more generous, more disciplined, more kind, more forgiving, more authentic, more mindful, more compassionate? More "woke," as the millennials would say? At what point would you say, "I have accomplished these qualities; I am content; I am satisfied"?

We're really trying to balance aspiration, ambition, effort, and accomplishment, with a sense of reasonableness, ease, and satisfaction. Of course, some of the most inspiring role models we might chose—the Buddha, Steve Jobs, Malala Yousafzai, Pablo Picasso, Frida Kahlo, Abraham Lincoln, Ruth Bader Ginsburg, Oprah Winfrey, Barack Obama, Elizabeth Warren, Jesus, Stephen Hawking, Serena or Venus Williams, or Mother Teresa—could be seen as powerfully driven (each in their own way) and very ambitious.

But they followed their path, and now it's our turn.

CONTENTMENT

The Buddha, who renounced worldly "success," set his sights even higher. He wasn't going to stop until he attained total, complete enlightenment—perhaps the loftiest goal possible.

He worked so hard. He tried very extreme ascetic practices. He allegedly got down to eating one grain of rice per day. He tried denying his sense perceptions, engaging in extreme yogic practices such as breath and body manipulation.

What he was after was for his struggle to cease. He was struggling to stop struggling! What he discovered in the end—and there are many different takes on what enlightenment is or isn't—has been described as a kind of indestructibly peaceful quality of being called nirvana, based on the cessation of struggle and suffering.

There's a very significant and often told story of the Buddha in the peak of his effort and aspiration. He was practicing so hard to release himself from samsara—the cycle of habitual patterns leading to repeatedly manifesting the same circumstances, psychological terrain, and even physical realities. At a certain point, he had a flash memory of himself as a child, happily playing in the fields, perhaps watched by a loving nanny—an effortless and natural situation of joy, carefree play, and delight.

According to the story, his mind, which had become drenched in effort and exertion, simply relaxed and opened. He was able to return to his effort in the practice of meditation, but with a lighter touch. He had discovered the now famous Middle Way. As a pith instruction from my teacher and my lineage puts it: "Not too tight and not too loose."

BTW, this moment of the Buddha's journey was the inspiration for my CD with the Beyman Bros (Christopher Guest, CJ Vanston, and myself) called *Memories of Summer as a Child*. Here's a URLs to a couple of free videos—relevant but also shameless plugs (as promised!): davidnichtern.com/beyman

And here's a link to streaming or downloading the album, if you're so inspired and in case you need a break from all this heavy thinking! davidnichtern.com/memories

We need to stop struggling and keep aspiring—seemingly an oxymoron. I have a trick I use: if I feel I'm leaning forward too far, I pull back; and if I feel I'm pulling back too hard, I lean in. For me, success is all about balance. It's like having a good gyroscope.

Not too tight and not too loose.

4 Surviving versus Thriving

My mission in life is not merely to survive, but to thrive;
and to do so with some passion, some compassion,
some humor, and some style.

—MAYA ANGELOU

WHEN OUR HEALTH or our life is threatened, we often pull back from creating and manifesting our vision and return to the fundamental instinct of life itself: the struggle to survive. Survival is so basic—without it, the rest of this conversation is moot. But developing our capacity to survive does not, of itself, necessarily lead to *thriving*.

Survival skills help us understand that life is fragile and impermanent, and that we need strength, power, and courage to get through the challenge of even a single day of living here on earth. They give us a competitive edge for our singular adventure and come with an acute awareness of scarcity—food, water, gasoline, shelter, clothing, money, etc. These resources are all limited, and for our survival we need to master acquiring them and managing our access to them.

Thriving, however, has an entirely different basis; it's accompanied by an awareness of abundance as opposed to scarcity. When we begin to thrive, we recognize that we've already survived and that we are in fact in a rich field of resources and opportunities. We can begin to acknowledge that we have a rich inheritance coming from our world, Mother Nature, our family, our cultural and spiritual lineage, our society, and in fact the *entire universe*, which from the point of view of thriving can be seen as a vast playground for us to inhabit and explore.

Ironically, some of the psychological and emotional skills that we learned in order to survive are exactly those that we'll need to release or transform in order to truly thrive. As we move into exploring creativity and livelihood skills, I think we'll see, over and over again, that our survival habits can become roadblocks on our highway to thriving. Some of them may need to be recognized, dismantled, and released.

To climb a ladder, we need to reach for and grasp the next rung while releasing our grip on the previous one. Developing our ability to let go actually helps us move toward success. In meditation, this is exactly the rhythm of our practice; we call it "touch and go."

"Touch and go" also describes the natural rhythm of life. By attuning to it, we can grow and evolve, which is the basis of genuine success. We can never achieve success and then just hold on to it for dear life. Reality doesn't work that way. There's always an element of letting go at every step of our journey.

"Surviving versus thriving" is more of a spectrum and a process of gradual development than a clearly delineated, black-and-white division. We're always somewhere along that spectrum, but we can also move backward and forward in real time—as in a game of Chutes and Ladders. For example, if we've begun to thrive, a health crisis or emergency could throw us back into our survival mode.

Let's go to your workbook.

6. Surviving versus Thriving

1. Write down three habits you've developed to help you survive, either in life or in business.
2. How might those habits block you from further growth? If they

do, how can they transform into a new approach that would enable you to move onward and upward in your journey?

3. What's your biggest threat to survival? What are you most afraid of?

4. What's your biggest obstacle to thriving as you understand the term?

Ironically, survival is the one battle we can never ultimately win. Eventually, as every one of us knows in our mind and heart, none of us will survive in the end. We will each die at some point in the future, and we have absolutely no idea when that event will occur. It's well worth contemplating this reality because it will give the life we have, and the precious time we have here on this beautiful earth, perspective and meaning.

It's important to understand survival, the required skill sets, and master them as much as possible. My father, who was a doctor, was big on emphasizing training in these skills. If we don't fully understand the notion of survival, we'll be vulnerable to collaborating with forces that can undermine our existence.

Ironically, in the end, my father, who was the guru of survival, succumbed to the ravages of Parkinson's disease and took his own life—in order to preserve the *quality* of his life. He was no longer thriving, so he decided to end his struggle. In so doing, I believe he was signaling that mere survival was no longer his primary objective.

In a powerful and controversial decision, his second wife also decided to take her life along with him. For her, thriving was clearly associated with being with my dad, and even though she was relatively healthy at the time, she opted for *nonsurviving*.

Of course, this book is intended to help each of us create a healthy relationship with our own survival, but the real thrust is to help us find our "thrive." This is a book about going beyond mere survival and manifesting something unique and powerful during the limited time we have here on earth.

5 Synchronicity and Uncle Irv

You should follow the dream that's also following you.
—PETE HOLMES, writer and star of the HBO series *Crashing*
and host of *You Made It Weird*

Both Buddhism and Taoism (as well as other wisdom traditions) have a way of holding opposites as a dynamic unity. In Taoism, as you might know, this duality is called *yin* and *yang*—seeming opposites that are intertwined and inseparable. In Middle Way Buddhism we describe reality as "not one and not two"; it's one of my favorite mind puzzles. This Middle Way approach also applies to our relationship to time.

Often our awareness is trapped in the past and the future. Our sharp, clear, awake mind can be clouded by doubt and regret, or dreamy reminiscing and nostalgia, emanating from our past. Our awareness can also get trapped in fear of a negative future or hope of a positive one.

When we find that sweet spot in the middle, a vivid feeling of *nowness* that resides between the past and the future, we can become very sensitive to the energy of the present moment. This kind of awareness is similar to what athletes and musicians (among others) call being *in the zone*. I think most of us have experienced and can recognize this timeless, effortless feeling of being synchronized internally and externally. We feel momentarily free of struggle and striving—almost magically, things seem to happen as they're meant to happen. What arises might feel relatively positive or negative, but everything somehow seems to be appropriate, workable, and serendipitous.

It's as if our instrument has been tuned; now it's much more ready to receive and resonate with sympathetic vibrations from other instruments. This type of resonance is built into the dynamic of our physical world and is easy to demonstrate with real musical instruments.

In Tibetan, this kind of synchronization is called *tendrel*, which means "auspicious coincidence," or synchronicity. Increased tendrel is often a byproduct of deep practice and is also said to be an important part of the atmosphere of advanced practitioners such as great teachers and masters. There's just more "coincidence power" around them.

On my friend Pete Holmes's podcast, *You Made It Weird*, I spontaneously started talking about the atmosphere of tendrel compared to the ordinary feeling of linear time, everyday mind, hope and fear, stress and anxiety, remorse and regret, as being like experiencing the energy of a 220-volt current as opposed to a 110-volt current (more intensity and more power): davidnichtern.com/tendrel

When we experience this kind of energy, it can remind us that the world we live in is a magical place. Look around and you'll see this to be true.

Nobody owns this magic and there's no way to copyright it. We simply tap into it—and then we let it go. This is an important proviso for when tendrel spontaneously happens: *we can just appreciate it and then let it go.* Any attempt to hold on to heightened states of meditation or life experiences can be counterproductive. CTR was adamant about this point; he even instructed us to "disown" them.

But tuning in to this kind of heightened feeling and synchronicity can, at times, be a key element for each of us to clarify our vision and make the right connections to manifest it.

Let's go to your workbook.

7. Synchronicity

1. Can you think of a time when your mind felt clear and open, you were synchronized in body and mind, and you experienced a sense of being in the zone?
2. Describe the situation in detail: How did you feel? How did your body feel? What was happening? What was the outcome?
3. Can you identify what pulled you out of the zone? Was there a reestablishing of anxiety or doubt as the governing element in the situation? What did that feel like?
4. What factors helped set the stage for your experience? Was there effort involved, or relaxation, or alcohol? Drugs? Romance? Inspiration from others? Special friends?
5. Can you recognize that there might be a kind of "coming down" from this feeling—like coming down from a drug experience or a great meeting or retreat? Could clinging to that heightened quality become problematic? Why or why not?

UNCLE IRV

Here I'm going to interject a personal story in order to illustrate this notion of synchronicity. The story centers on my deeply treasured Uncle Irv.

Irving Joseph was my real uncle—my mother's younger brother— even though some of my friends thought that Uncle Irv was his stage name. He was, in fact, a kind of cosmic uncle. At his memorial service many younger folks stepped up and said, "He was like an uncle to me."

When it was my turn to speak at his memorial service, I said, "Well, he was my *actual* uncle, but he was also *like* an uncle to me." And then I did my best to sing a song I wrote when my dad passed away and when CTR passed away, called "In My Heart and On My Mind," but I couldn't get all the way through it.

You can hear a lovely version of this song by my friend Elise Morris, with me playing acoustic guitar, here: davidnichtern.com/elise

Uncle Irv mentored me. He always took time to hang out and deeply listen, and he gave me so much great support and advice. Frankly, instead of "grandmother's advice," we could call the kind of guidance in this book "Uncle Irv's advice"—straight from the heart, laden with the rich fruits of deep experience of living, dotted with humor (many jokes in heavy rotation, but charming anyway).

So here are two stories about Uncle Irv that perhaps belong equally to the creativity section of this book, but I think you'll see why I decided to include them here.

Uncle Irv was a professional musician—my role model who confirmed that such a thing was even possible. He actually escorted me personally to Local 802 of the American Federation of Musicians, endorsed my application, and started me on the course of being legit and authorized to take your money for playing the guitar.

Uncle Irv was classically trained, but he was primarily a jazz musician. He toured with jazz legend Tommy Dorsey's band when he was just sixteen years old; played with Nina Simone and Frank Sinatra; conducted the touring company of *Jesus Christ Superstar*; accompanied his first wife, nightclub chanteuse Felicia Sanders; conducted and accompanied Patti LuPone for her nightclub act (while I was her guitarist and music director); and was conductor and accompanist for Rita Moreno for decades.

His touch on the piano was extraordinarily graceful. Somehow he was able to completely transcend the fact that the piano is actually a percussion instrument, and instead make it sound like water flowing in a river on a moonlit night—luminous and fluid. Not so easy to do.

In the 1990s my band was playing at a joint on the West Side of Manhattan called Wilson's. We'd just released a new album. Inspired by old friend Loudon Wainwright III's suggestion, it was titled—that's right, you guessed it—*From Here to Nichternity*.

Hey, here's a link to *From Here to Nichternity* while we're talking about it. Check it out: davidnichtern.com/album

Sometimes Uncle Irv would open for my band playing a cocktail/dinner set on solo piano. In my totally unbiased opinion, he was one of the greatest ever at playing standards medleyed together, smoothly morphing through song, key, and tempo changes, forming a seamless tapestry of familiarity and improvisation. He was just a genius at this art form.

So I had an idea: Why not record him creating a similar set for my 5 Points Records label? We could call the project *The Cocktail Hour* and sell it to the millions of people worldwide who have parties and don't have the extra shekels to hire live musicians. It seemed like a viable concept, creatively and commercially.

So we had Uncle Irv come into our recording studio in Manhattan, tuned up the grand piano there, and set out to make this recording. Our recording engineer was one of the people I mentioned earlier who didn't immediately realize that Irv was my real uncle; he thought Uncle Irv was his stage name.

Irv sat down at the piano, warmed up a bit, and then we went for what I thought would be "take 1." Usually the way this kind of session goes is that we stop and start a few times (at least), work out modulations, fix some mistakes, and then later edit everything together using our digital editing system.

Irv started to play. We listened carefully and happily as he wove his way through the entire program from beginning to end, complete with modulations and tempo changes—a beautiful selection and sequencing of thirty classic songs that everybody knows and loves. He never took his hands off the piano for about fifty-four minutes—at which point he lifted his hands from the piano, paused for a minute, looked up, and was done.

My mind and the engineer's mind were completely blown. There was the entire record. We might have recorded one alternative ending, but I don't think we used it. It was perfect as it was. He just warmed up, stepped into the zone, and came out fifty-four minutes later—the album was complete.

I think we should add that a lifetime of preparation allowed Uncle Irv this amount of access to the flow. But this recording session is a great example of that quality of synchronizing body and mind, and accessing the space in which communication is effortless and perfect as it is. I sometimes thought of him as a kind of Taoist master of the piano. He was a true maestro.

My second Uncle Irv story illustrates another point we'll keep bumping into throughout this book: the notion of impermanence and the need to let go or even "disown" (as per CTR's instructions) any attachment we might have to a particular outcome—related to either our meditation experience or our experience of life itself. We can never really hold on to anything.

Contemplate Impermanence

Take your meditation seat and bring your mind to this topic, exploring it fully and personally for five minutes.

Each time you do so will be different. There are no right or wrong contemplations. Just mix your mind with the topic and keep coming back to it when you wander. Don't settle for formulaic answers. Each time you contemplate, see how far into the topic you can reach and then keep going further.

When your mind wanders, just gently bring your thoughts back to the contemplation.

Uncle Irv, as I mentioned previously, was classically trained, but he'd spent the majority of his working life as a jazz pianist. He had mastery of a certain part of the classical piano repertoire but had never really performed in that genre, which is technically very demanding.

As he approached the tender age of seventy-five, he aspired to create his first "classical" concert at a recital hall in New York. He booked the hall, created a program, had my sister Nicky design a very nice written program for the dates, and began practicing the music five hours a day for several months.

He was totally excited to be meeting this challenge. Some would have considered these his senior years, but they'd more accurately be described as his peak years; his training, life experience, and effort were all coming together in a beautiful climax, and I so, so respected him for this effort. Put this in your pipe and smoke it the next time you feel you're too fried or too used up to turn on your lightsaber, mount up, and ride your magical windhorse into the golden dawn.

But there was a twist. Irv got sick and then sicker. At first, he, like most of us would, felt as if this was an illness that would pass, but his health began to rapidly decline. The next thing I knew we were visiting him at the NYU medical center. As each day passed he got weaker and weaker. I spent as much time as possible in his hospital room.

It was one of the few times I gave "ear-whispered" instructions to someone, as it became clearer and clearer that he was passing away. I told him not to be afraid and to view whatever appeared to him as reflections of his own mind's projections. I told him to let go of this very life, which he had lived so elegantly, so beautifully, and just move onward. At some point he looked up at me and said, "I am leaving the magic circle." Those were his exact words.

Uncle Irv never did get to play that classical concert.

The Cocktail Hour was later put out by another record company and renamed *I Love a Piano—30 Great American Hits*. If you'd like to invite a few friends over and have a couple of drinks and some good conversation about this cool new book you're reading, this music is highly recommended!

And here's a link to Uncle Irv's *I Love a Piano*:
davidnichtern.com/irv

As for me, I have a hard time listening to it; to me, it's perfect and that's joyful but also painful. I'm still working on letting go of Uncle Irv.

Part II Getting Down to Business

WHEN THE BUDDHA was asked to verify his enlightenment, he simply touched the earth and the earth shook in response. This gesture is generally considered to represent the quality of being fully grounded—of being absolutely present to be able to communicate with reality *as it is.*

You could say that this understanding is somewhat the opposite of the notion of spirituality as some kind of transcendent, etheric, abstract knowledge that has nothing to do with life on earth. In fact, sometimes CTR would talk about Dharma as being transcendental *common sense.*

Since our view here is that how we conduct our business isn't separate from our most profound wisdom, I would like to link this image of the Buddha touching the earth with the notion of getting down to business—entering the field of activity (busyness) from an "enlightened" perspective. Business can be an essential spiritual practice; it gives us the opportunity, in the tangible realm, to express and manifest our most closely held values and beliefs. In turn, we can learn some of life's most powerful lessons—direct and raw—without any kind of philosophical or metaphysical padding.

Remember, we're not advocating becoming the greediest stuffed pig on the planet here—where's the grace in that? We're talking about having a balanced and healthy existence.

6 Clarify Your Offering

Make something delicious for someone you love.
—DAVE ELLNER, founder of Panna (www.pannacooking.com)
and former CFO of Universal Music Group

WHEN WE CONTEMPLATE heaven and earth, remember that there's a third important component in this relationship: humanity. In this traditional view, the job of humans is to join heaven and earth—to bring together vision and practicality. As we focus our exploration, I think we'll begin to see that we each have some kind of special offering to make to this world. Perhaps this approach is kind of romantic, and if so, I can live with that.

If we see our existence as some kind of fundamental expression of creativity, it's only natural to conclude that we can and should express ourselves, if only in the spirit of call and response; the universe created us and now we're responding by creating our offering back. Our offering could be art, business, charity, leadership, innovation—that's entirely up to each one of us. We can have a variety of offerings, even a plethora of offerings. The notion here is that we each have some unique expression, idea, presentation that we're inspired to bring out of our inner world and present to our outer world: our family, friends, colleagues, community, society, world, even universe, if you want to reach that far.

At this point we're just trying to *feel*, to *assess*, what we want to express from our unique perspective. In the next section, if we choose, we're going to see what's involved with presenting our offering beyond our intimate world of family and friends; we're going to explore sharing our offering with the larger world: our community, society, and beyond. Here, though, we're just trying to access our personal Geiger counter and see what we naturally tune in to, what intrigues us, what we enjoy communicating with and about—in essence, what floats our boat.

For example, as mentioned, I'm a guitar player. I started to play when I was eight years old. My older sister, Nicky, got the piano lessons, so I got the guitar. Sometimes, as a composer, producer, and arranger, I wish I had gotten the piano lessons, but as my mom used to say, "If my grandmother had wheels, she'd be a wagon"—I think you can grok the meaning. That's just how it was. Anyway, the guitar has been a constant companion since then. The guitar and music in general have been and will be for the foreseeable future an important part of my communication portal with the world. It's definitely a major part of my offering.

I would say that my second love affair in this life has been with the Buddhist teachings, my teacher, and my community—we call those the "three jewels," and that's actually how I feel about them. I got interested in Buddhism in college, and I met my teacher when I was around twenty-two. From then on, Buddhist studies and practice became a second major aspect of my life in this world.

Many people play guitar their whole lives for the fun of it, and many people study and practice Buddhism for their own development without becoming teachers. So it's important to note that in regard to both of these powerful interests, I went beyond personal involvement and made them part of my offering back to the big world.

Throughout my life, these two offerings have vied for my time, attention, and bandwidth. And to some extent, that's still the case today. I simply don't have the bandwidth to work intensively on both at the same time. For example, I'm putting aside my work on a new musical for the moment while I write this book. I'm also playing guitar a bit less frequently with my friend Krishna Das so I can go around the world and teach meditation workshops and teacher trainings. I can only be in one place at one time.

For me, because I have diverse interests and offerings, integration has become important. If I were counseling myself, I might say, "David, your offering is too diverse. It will confuse people—and maybe even you. Pick one area of expertise and focus on it completely for the greatest success." But if I did that, I wouldn't be being me. Our offering has to come from a real assessment of who we are. It has to be genuine; it has to be authentic. I'm genuinely eclectic. It's who I am, so I have to go with it.

I also have a third thread: I love the entrepreneurial spirit. I think I'm a real American in that way—take a great idea and create an empire. From a creative point of view, how cool is that?

So for me, my job is to weave together these three threads: create art (music), learn about life and help people, and bring it to the box office. There's no venture that I'm currently involved with that doesn't have some variation of this blend at its root. I mean, look at the topic of this book! My life has finally become simple, even though it can appear intricate and complex. This weave is my offering, and from my point of view, that's totally clear.

For you, your offering can be as yet undiscovered, or discovered but not ripened (think of a green banana or a hard melon), or ripened but not yet fully manifested and shared. It could be as a marketing person, a salesperson, a scientist, a theoretical physicist, a pharmacist, an elementary school teacher, a lifestyle innovator, an architect, a garbage collector, a short-order cook—whatever.

Let's go to your workbook.

📖 8. Clarify Your Offering

1. Contemplate and define your offering in a general sense.
2. Then, get specific: What's unique about you? Why are you uniquely qualified to make this particular offering?
3. What contribution would you like to make to others? Family? Community? Society?
4. Is your main offering how you make your living? If not, would you like it to be? If so, how is that going so far: Well, or could it be better? (If the latter, hopefully the next section will be helpful!) ✎

7 Take Your Offering to the Marketplace

But yield who will to their separation,
My object in living is to unite
My avocation and my vocation
As my two eyes make one in sight.
Only where love and need are one,
And the work is play for mortal stakes . . .
  —ROBERT FROST, "Two Tramps in Mud Time"

FOR SOME of us, our offering may come from a deep passion, perhaps one we want to preserve in its purity—we don't want to bring our livelihood concerns into the picture.

Charles Ives, for example, felt this way. He was a major American composer in the early twentieth century, and he sold life insurance (very successfully, apparently) so he wouldn't have to concern himself with the commercial aspects of being a composer. Many painters, filmmakers, musicians, craftspeople, chefs, etc., may feel the same way about their offering. That's fine!

However, if we see our day job as simply an enabler for some other activity—if we can't see our work as *some* kind of offering—our life could easily start to feel static and uninspiring. All of us have to take some kind of offering to the marketplace, even if only to be able to pay our rent and other bills. I encourage you to find the value in whatever it is that you spend your day doing—to find the offering in your job.

Some people keep their job and their calling separate. Others migrate toward a more holistic relationship between their passion and their work life. Some folks, as they clarify their offering, move onward and upward. Others find that downsizing might create the right balance. Hopefully the general principles discussed in the chapters in part 2 will apply to any and all business situations, helping you move toward balance, productivity, and efficiency.

So now let's come back to our offering (whether it's our heart song or our day job) and begin to explore how we can take it to the marketplace and create a viable livelihood from it.

1. Define Your Offering

> **The first step is to clearly define your offering.** It can be a service, a product, or intellectual property. It comes from who you are, what you're good at, and what you create in your life to present to others.

Some of us, particularly in the earlier part of our lives, might have inherited a strong notion of what our offering *should* be, based on parents, peers, or society. I went to Columbia College (at the tender age of sixteen) without any clue as to what my livelihood would look like. My dad was a doctor. Good gig: good money, good values . . . why not? I registered as a premedical student with an English minor. Later I realized that the medical profession was a complete overlay for me—it didn't really come from the core, so to speak—and I dropped out of premed, took on English and creative writing as my major, and perhaps most significantly kept up with my personal passion: playing guitar and being in various bands.

I was still under the sway of my parents and society, which at the time were both saying, "What are you, nuts? It's impossible to make a living as a musician. Have a fallback. Be a doctor—that's honorable, credible, and a solid livelihood." From their point of view, being a doctor was the "right" course. But it wasn't the right answer for me, and I had to find out for myself what was.

At the time, one of the bands I played in was with my buddy Christopher Guest, my only soup-to-nuts lifetime friend. (My mother introduced his parents to each other, and we were born two weeks apart, seventy years ago.) Our band was called Voltaire's Nose, and we played covers and originals at various frat parties and the like. So there I was playing music, as I had been for years, but it hadn't yet occurred to me that music could be my actual *offering*, let alone my livelihood.

To find your offering will take some searching, some experimenting, some success, some failure, some feedback, some inspiration, sometimes even some pigheadedness and determination against all odds.

2. LINK YOUR CREATIVE OFFERING TO YOUR LIVELIHOOD OFFERING

> The need to create may be a personal one—but for your creation to serve a market or an audience, you must **be aware of the needs of others.**

Aware of the needs of others? You mean there *are* others? What a concept! Sometimes creative types in particular have little awareness of the existence of others, let alone what others think about, care about, or need. But if we're going to bring our goodies to the marketplace, we have to tune in to what's going on around us.

For example, Chris and I loved to play rock-and-roll together, but to monetize our goofy little project I had to reach out to college fraternities and dances and try to get us booked as the entertainment for their events. And people wanted to *dance* at those parties, so we didn't play bluegrass (which we often have); we played dance music—and mostly songs they were already familiar with.

Of course, that's just a tiny example of this principle. As our creativity expands, we might find that we're able to create something original that we love, and the audience grows and follows along with us. But even so, we have to be aware of the audience and connect with them.

If we're producing comedies and nobody finds them funny, we'll run out of producers, backers, and audience sooner than later. Obviously that didn't happen with Chris, who was able to create from his own unique comedic aesthetic and find his now substantial audience. There's still, however, the principle that he, and other creatives, must be in sync with some unique gathering of kindred spirits who are willing to pay the price of a ticket. Otherwise, even geniuses won't be able to keep creating—unless they're independently wealthy or have an . . . ugh . . . day job.

There are myriad jokes about this kind of thing in the musician world. For example: What did the tuba player say at his gig? The answer: "Do you want fries with that shake?" I think you get the idea. We might be deeply interested in something like jazz for tuba ensembles, and there may not seem to be too much of a need or market for that. But oops, oh yes, my friend Howard Johnson did exactly that and *did* find a modest but cool audience for his offering. Howard was one tuba player who could say at his gig, "This one's in B-flat, and it goes something like this."

This goes to show that there are no hard-and-fast rules here, but regardless, some awareness of the landscape is always helpful.

3. Continuously Refine Your Offering

> Your offering should be the best it can possibly be.
> **Refining your offering will require effort and energy.**

This one can be painful. Sometimes when we read that hard work is going to be a factor, that there's no fast track or instant magic—at that exact moment we might decide to put this book down and reach for our remote control or cell phone.

But there's no way around it. Our offering might be pretty hot at one moment, and three months later it might be perceived as old hat. And we're not just talking about keeping up with the trends here; we're encouraging the time-honored virtues of hard work and honing our skills as a matter of personal pride. Even if we become masters, we should always remain students. We should never rest on our laurels.

4. Know Your Market / Do Your Homework

In order for your offering to meet the marketplace, you should **know your market**, have some idea of its size, and know how to communicate with the people in that market.

I admit it—I love the TV show *Shark Tank*. Some of the questions the judges always ask are the same questions that any successful entrepreneur is going to ask: "What is the market for your offering? What is the size of that market? And what will your customer acquisition cost be?" (That is, how much will it cost you to get a potential customer in that market segment to actually acquire your product or services?) These are really, really good questions.

In response, so many inexperienced entrepreneurs will tout the virtues, the brilliance, the glistening, the magic—the buzz around their offering—and this is a dead giveaway that they haven't done their homework and assessed the existing or potential marketplace. You can skip this step and get lucky, but that puts you in the gambling business. Well, actually, not even—good gamblers don't just close their eyes, throw the dice, and pray for the best. They have some idea of the rules of the game, underlying principles, and the odds for success. Do your homework!

5. SOME OFFERINGS WILL CREATE THEIR OWN MARKET; OTHERS ARE DESIGNED FOR EXISTING MARKETS

**Some offerings come out of your personal creativity.
Others are designed to meet a specific market need**
(such as creating a can opener once cans have hit the market).

Oh, *this* is an interesting topic. Our offering can be content driven or market driven. Both are completely workable premises, but they're not necessarily interchangeable.

Putting out a new hip-hop record is placing a product into an existing marketplace. You're banking that there's something compelling and special about your offering, but you won't have to reinvent the marketplace. People know what hip-hop is and they're *already looking* for the next iteration.

But putting out the first hip-hop record is another story—"Hip what?" You have to be a leader, a visionary, a great communicator. Often this can be a steep and winding road to travel, but the payoff, creatively and commercially, can be vastly rewarding. Think Steve Jobs and Wozniak and Apple. Nobody even knew what a personal computer was, what it did, or why we would need one. Personally, I love the process of trying to communicate the inherent value of something that hasn't yet reached a particular marketplace—or any marketplace.

These days the previously niche offering of meditation is being brought to the mainstream, and it's such an interesting process to observe and participate in. At first people will try to make it feel familiar—it helps us strengthen our focus, it reduces stress and anxiety, it's backed by the findings of good old neuroscience. All these things are true. But wait . . . there's more!

Meditation might also change our lives in unpredictable ways. We might rediscover thoughts and emotions that we had locked away for decades. We might have all kinds of insights and game-changing shifts of perspective. We might develop empathy and compassion for others beyond the level of productivity and efficiency.

Compassion can sometimes be a barrier to productivity and efficiency, as we realize that what we all really need is to slow down and take more time to appreciate ourselves, others, and our environment. Meditation can and *has*, in the past, transformed entire societies.

So when we present meditation as an offering, we have to be aware of its full range and then target whomever we want to be communicating with about it—whether that be corporations, fitness companies, yogis, leaders, creatives, etc. It's not a one-size-fits-all situation. We still have to know our audience.

6. DON'T SPREAD YOURSELF TOO THIN

If your time and energy are spread too thinly across a variety of (possibly wonderful) offerings, some or all of them may falter.

I could write a whole other book on this topic. Maybe it could be called "How to Spread Yourself—Not Too Thick and Not Too Thin." It's funny to be the peanut butter and also the knife that spreads it on the bread. But we all have to make decisions about where to invest our time and energy, and we all most likely feel that we are, at times, making difficult choices between family, work, play, ongoing education, new adventures, and the various offerings we're contemplating.

An abundance of activities and engagements isn't necessarily a curse, but we may need to be mindful about having too many bets running at too many tables, especially when it comes to our livelihood. We may find that we need to balance our creativity with focus and practical considerations.

Now let's go to your workbook again.

9. Take Your Offering to Market

1. What's your primary offering? If it's also your livelihood offering, how have you gone about presenting it as such? Please answer with adjustments you have made in framing or formulating the content and in learning and executing marketing and sales strategies for that particular arena.

2. What obstacles have you faced in transforming your creative output into a livelihood vehicle? For instance: your own impatience, lack of required skills, lack of support from others, etc.

3. How did you overcome (or attempt to overcome) those obstacles?

4. What advice would you give to the rest of us about this process? What have you learned that would be valuable to share with others?

8 The Anatomy of the Business Body

A COO needs to be able to see the entire picture . . . to recognize that every spoke in the wheel is ultimately as important as the other. So the individual in the warehouse who is receiving and packing and shipping—their ability is as important as the person on the road selling, doing the marketing, or the person who's looking after the books.

—MICHAEL MAYZEL, cofounder of Lowepro International and partner of Blue Spirit Retreat Center (Costa Rica)

BEFORE WE DIVE into planning, executing, and all that, let's take a look at some fundamentals of business systems.

Just like any other area of our lives, business has some grounding principles. Sometimes people get lucky and create a phenomenal offering at just the right time, and somehow magically all the elements come together and create a huge wave of prosperity. Even in a blessed situation like that, the whole enterprise can still go right off the rails if we don't understand and execute the fundamentals. Like an heiress squandering a huge fortune, a star athlete going bankrupt, or a new company going out of business because they're unable to generate enough cash flow to finance a necessary expansion, we still may falter along the way.

With this more disciplined approach in mind, let's look at the anatomy of the business body. There are five elements—and just like in a human body, each has to be developed individually, and they all have to be working together for our business enterprise to be truly successful.

1. The Heart Is Your Offering

We've talked about our offering quite a bit already. Here I liken it to the heart of the business body, because it's the vital engine at the center of the whole operation, generating energy and radiating out.

2. The Legs Are R&D and Product Development

As discussed in chapter 7, the formulation and creation of your offering, whether it's goods or services, is the foundation of being in business—hence, the legs. One leg is content development, sometimes called R&D for "research and development," and the other leg is fashioning that content into a tangible product. What content are you going to develop and what are you going to sell?

Your company, from small to big, has to commit to ongoing exploration to create and refine your content. Let us call that the left leg. For example, in the music business, record companies have special staff whose main role is to locate, attract, and develop talent. They do their research, their homework: they find out who is out playing and creating an offering and an audience.

The company then has to put that creative talent together with the right support team—producers, managers, agents—who can help fashion that artist into a product. (I know this sounds crass when it comes to the arts, but it's true when it comes to the business component.) If you're a musician, this is when you create the CD, digital downloads, live concerts, video, merchandise, etc., etc. Let's call this aspect the right leg: transforming your creation into a tangible, definable product. What is it, how much does it cost to make, and what will you sell it for?

3. THE ARMS ARE SALES AND MARKETING

Sales and marketing are the arms of your business. Your left arm is marketing: how you reach out, communicate with your world, and pass out information about your product. Your right arm is sales: the one you use to distribute your product and collect the money from anybody who is willing to pay to own it. You can reverse the arms if you're a lefty!

In our record company analogy, the marketing people create a plan to help connect the artist with their potential audience—to let people know they exist, what their offering is, and what products are currently available for purchase. Marketing can include print and media ads, PR, and social media—among a variety of other options to get the word out.

The sales force then sets up the appropriate distribution channels to move the products into the hands of the consumer and collect the revenue. Obviously marketing and sales have to operate in tandem, so the demand created synchronizes with the capacity to distribute the product and fill orders in a timely fashion.

Please note that although we haven't assigned them a particular body part herein, if your company creates tangible goods, manufacturing and distribution will be part of the equation too. Many companies will have a special department and manager to oversee manufacturing, but distribution will often be part of the sales department's purview.

Digital media has changed the game here to some extent, as the product can remain online in perpetuity with no additional carrying cost to the manufacturer. This model has created what's now known as the *long tail*: a dramatic extension of the shelf life of music, books, video, and other media. But the basic principles of letting people know that your product exists and is desirable, and making sure it's readily available, are still where the rubber hits the road in your business model.

4. THE BRAIN IS ADMINISTRATION

I wish I had a dollar for every time I've seen somebody who is bright, talented, well meaning, who basically has a great idea—and seen them act as if they don't know where their brain is. Many parents have felt this way about their teenage children, who are also apparently bright, talented, and fundamentally well meaning.

The brain, or head, of your business body is the administration; it pulls all the elements of your business together. The different aspects need to be recognized, respected, communicated with, and properly synchronized. Just as your brain directs your body in the literal sense, the brain of your business body directs and coordinates the heart, legs, and arms of your business body, creating and refining your plan and bringing your limbs together in harmony to execute that plan.

As the demand for recorded music grew dramatically in the '60s and '70s, record companies found themselves moving from an entrepreneurial style of operation to a more corporate model. Accountants, lawyers, and executives in charge of administration became more and more critical to the success of these rapidly growing companies. We used to call these people "the suits," because they were in stark contrast to the more bohemian style of the hipsters who had started these companies and the people who had found and created the superstars whose success fueled the labels.

These suits are often necessary, even vital, to a business. Every body needs a healthy brain! But it's important that the brain stays in touch with all other aspects of the body and doesn't take over too strongly. For example, one of the outcomes of bringing in the suits in the record business is that at a certain point, because they're expert in analyzing and understanding sales figures and trends, they begin to take over the operating positions in these now mega corporations. You find yourself sending music to lawyers and accountants to pitch your product to them. And they're making decisions about whether or not the music is high quality and will be appealing to large or niche audiences. I don't want to generalize too much, but they're not necessarily (with some notable exceptions) the best qualified to take over this function.

What's really at issue here is a potential stress point, as an entrepreneurial venture grows, between creativity and making a buck. Creativity seems to drive the early stages of business and then, as the system gets larger, as a company develops investors and stockholders, it's possible that the admin people take over.

At that point, it's also possible that the company loses its creative shape and direction. You might then begin to see either a decline in the energy and vitality of the company, or a kind of continuing success based on staying with the existing product lines—but without further innovation. In essence the company loses its heart and the brain takes over.

This kind of evolution can also happen in our spiritual and emotional life if our brain takes over and we lose track of our heart and creativity. It's about balance.

5. The Ears Are Customer Service

If you succeed but don't listen to or take care of your customers properly, sooner or later your business will wobble and crash.

A great business should have talented people and a well-organized system dedicated to customer service. Your customers are your lifeline. You want them to be happy and talking to other people about what a cool company you have.

In our record company model, the ears would be equivalent to reaching out to your customers and finding out what, if anything, they enjoy about your offering, and being fluid and updating your output accordingly.

Of course, sometimes the customers demand the same old, same old. This is an easy trap to fall into; it's hard for great artists to resist the temptation to simply reproduce their greatest hits. I'm certainly not telling you to stop innovating. But listening to your customers is different than simply giving them what they think they want over and over again. So here again is the balance between being creative (output) and being sensitive to the needs of the marketplace (input). If your offering is your livelihood, in most instances you'll need both—more about all this in our creativity section.

If you look at your business using the analogy of the business body, it might give you a clearer perspective as to why and how your business will succeed or fail. If one part of your business body isn't working well, it will affect the others—immediately, sooner, or later.

I've seen many entrepreneurs flounder because they didn't understand, appreciate, or even worse, *like* one or more of these essential components of the business body. Most commonly, perhaps, we see the creative entrepreneur or artist who doesn't enjoy admin or sales and marketing. That can be a big problem for them. They then have to either hire someone to run their company or just stay frustrated and irritated by the cascade of details, bills, and negotiations that begin to take up all their time.

A friend of mine started a commercial recording studio, as a business but also in order to have his own facility to create his personal musical offering. The outcome was (and often is in that kind of situation) predictable: he ended up bumping himself from the studio to bring in paying clients because he needed revenue to keep the doors open. He actually had to build a second, smaller studio behind the first one for his use only and hire a full-time professional manager to take over the responsibilities of running his now completely commercialized studio.

Another problem I've often seen is that most businesses start small, just like a baby, and then—gods willing—they grow bigger in stages. In the earliest stages, especially in the world of the entrepreneur, there may be only one single person—*you*—fulfilling all these different roles, wearing every hat and basically going crazy trying to accomplish all those functions. If you're lucky you might have a mom, pop, husband, wife, kids, or friends who lean in and lend a hand. If your company makes it through these early stages of its evolution, then you'll start to pass out those hats to a variety of individuals who have different skill sets than you have. You'll begin to differentiate the different parts of the business body.

At this point, you'll have to be able to recognize and appreciate the different kinds of toolboxes people come with and be willing to compensate them appropriately. If you can't, one of the limbs of your company, and ultimately your whole company, will suffer.

Sometimes entrepreneurs, who loved the start-up excitement of getting their little baby out into the world and moving around, become disenchanted as their baby starts to grow up. Some of them will crave those earlier days of chaos and fertility and choose to sell their stake in their growing business and start all over again.

Many of you reading this book will probably fall into the more entre-preneurial style of person, but the toolboxes offered here should be equally applicable to the entrepreneur and to the valuable and skilled employee, for your spiritual evolution, your well-being, your creativity, and mastering your livelihood, at whatever level you aspire to operate.

Now let's get back to you—please go to your workbook.

10. The Body of Your Business

1. If you're an entrepreneur, write a little about the different aspects of the business body as you're experiencing them. Can you identify the parts you enjoy and the parts that are more of a struggle for you?
2. Even if you're now employed by or have previously worked for a large and established company, can you talk about the

issues that came up regarding communication between the different parts of the company?

3. When you work for others, where do you find yourself fitting into the business body of that company? What problems, if any, do you find recurring for you within that context?

4. Please feel free to comment about any aspect of the discussion in this chapter as it relates to your understanding of the business body and your relationship to it, whether past, present, or heading into a possible future adventure you're contemplating.

9 Vision, Plan, Execution
Ground, Path, and Fruition

A goal without a timeline is simply a dream.
—ROBERT HERJAVEC, star of *Shark Tank*

WHEN I LEARNED how to teach Buddhism from Chögyam Trungpa Rinpoche, he repeatedly emphasized structuring our teaching on what he called *ground, path, and fruition*—also sometimes called *view, practice, and action* or *threefold logic*.

Simply put, the *ground* is our basis, our starting point. The ground of this book, for example, is that I wanted to share my life's journey and experience, express myself fully, and help others along the way as much as possible.

With that intention in mind, I then entered the second leg of the experience: *path*, or practice. There's a journey to make, and exertion, discipline, and effort are required. To create this book, I had to spend hundreds of hours writing and organizing, rewriting and reorganizing this material. It was fun, but it was *work*. The path is like the part of a marathon when we dig in hard in order to stay the course and execute our full intention.

In every path (and every marathon, for that matter), we'll probably reach what I call the "two-thirds-through moment." In this moment, we can no longer remember why we started, and the end is nowhere in sight. Runners call this "hitting the wall." We all can relate to that description. Hitting the wall is part of every journey. At that point we simply have to persevere and stay the course.

If we keep to our path through thick and thin, dark and light, up and down, right and wrong, weak and strong, good and bad, happy and sad, juiced and fried, then and only then will we experience the *fruition*, or result, of that journey. We'll have reached our destination. In the case of spiritual practice, it could mean that we've achieved wisdom, power, insight, clarity, and peace. In business it could mean wealth, satisfaction, benefit for ourselves, and benefit for others.

Ask anybody who has ever written a book, built a building, planted a garden, composed a symphony, gone to law school, cleaned their apartment, had a relationship, or lived a full life, and they will know what we're talking about here. We plant a seed; we nurture, water, and prune the tree; and then we can eat the fruit that it bears.

Trungpa Rinpoche would encourage us to use this model of ground, path, and fruition as a way to structure our thinking—particularly in relation to preparing to teach others. He would drill us on developing our threefold logic as a way to focus and structure our presentation on any Dharma topic.

For example, here's a simple ground-path-and-fruition structure regarding why we might consider mindfulness meditation. If the "why" (ground) isn't clear to us, and if we can't make it clear to others (path), nobody would ever do this practice. The ground has to be clear and the path has to be illuminated, otherwise the fruition will be elusive at best.

Ground: Because my mind is easily distracted and jumps around like a frog on steroids.

Path: I'm practicing mindfulness by bringing my attention back, over and over again, to a single stimulus (such as the breath).

Fruition: Through this cultivation of mindfulness meditation, my mind has become clearer, more focused, and more stable.

This is a very simple analytical process, but it allows us to clarify the basis of meditation—or any other kind of process or activity.

Let's see if we can apply this same process to our livelihood. Having created this particular template of ground, path, and fruition, as we shift into the context of our business ventures, the threefold logic becomes this:

Ground: Define your vision and create a plan.

Path: Execute the plan, adapting as necessary.

Fruition: The check is in the mail.

Here are some examples of the threefold logic applied to general business contexts:

Ground: Because I need to make more money to support my family and upgrade our lifestyle, I prepare for a conversation with my employer.

Path: I lay out the reasons I think I deserve a raise (he's staring, I'm sweating).

Fruition: 1. They agreed, and I got my raise.
2. They laughed in my face and now I'm brushing up my resume ☺.

The fruition of one leg of our journey naturally becomes the ground for the next leg. In the example above, the ground that would follow the second option would probably begin "I need to find a job."

However, if we're able to create prosperity in our business, the next leg could go like this:

Ground: Use the engine of existing success.

Path: Stabilize revenues and administration.

Fruition: Achieve an atmosphere of harmony, productivity, and efficiency.

Or, alternatively:

Ground: Use the engine of existing success.

Path: Reinvest resources in expanding opportunities.

Fruition: The company grows.

Get the idea?

So I'm going to use a business venture I was involved with a few decades ago as an example. Here's the story.

NEW ENGLAND DIGITAL (THE SYNCLAVIER ADVENTURE)

In 1978, I was living in a beautiful house on Mulholland Drive in Los Angeles, newly married to my first wife, Janice, with the baby Ethan in the "oven."

Ethan's the real maestro Dharma teacher in this family. Check him out here: davidnichtern.com/ethan

At this point, I'd been living in LA for four years as a songwriter, guitarist, film composer, and record producer. I'd written a fun little song called "Midnight at the Oasis," and then I'd had the opportunity to record it with a singer I was working with as guitarist and bandleader—Maria Muldaur. Somehow this little ditty went supernova and became a major international hit record. Hits were then, and are still now, the major currency and lubricant of the music business, so for a while I was in fat city for cash and in demand for my services—a dream situation for a struggling musician.

Then I was asked by my Buddhist teacher if my new little family and I could move to the Karmê Chöling Meditation Center in Barnet, Vermont, where I would become the new codirector.

The center was growing and needed a director with real-world experience, a "grown-up" to help shepherd the center into a more professional manifestation that would enable many more people to study and practice the Dharma there. It's a funny tribute to the times (the '70s) that I, thirty years old and basically a hippie-musician type, was the closest thing we could find to a grown-up in our rapidly evolving community. Most of us were in our twenties and thirties—CTR himself was only thirty-nine—and the times were a bit wild and edgy. As the famous quote goes, "If you can remember Woodstock, then you weren't there." That kind of thing.

If you haven't heard "Midnight at the Oasis" or haven't heard it recently—grab yourself a falafel and have a listen: davidnichtern.com/oasis

In any case, Janice squeezed out the baby Ethan, we closed up our big beautiful house in LA, moved a few belongings into two tiny rooms at Karmê Chöling, and started a whole new chapter of our lives. It was intense.

This was a powerful and difficult time in my attempt to integrate my spiritual practice with my worldly existence. We went from living in a luxurious setting in the Hollywood Hills into what was basically two of the larger closets in our old house. I went from making hundreds of thousands of dollars a year with bright prospects to earning twenty-five dollars per week plus room and board! And by the end of my tenure at Karmê Chöling, I had effectively lost most of the momentum I had accumulated in my music career. I had a wife, a baby, and a whole different set of responsibilities. It occurred to me that I might actually need—ugh!—a job.

In the field of tendrel (synchronicity), I made a seemingly innocent foray to a company called New England Digital (NED), which had been founded by a member of the greater Karmê Chöling community—Syd Alonso. At the time, Syd was an old-timey fiddle player, kind of rough-hewn in a charming way, and hardly a person I thought would be the inventor and designer of what would become, without doubt, the leading edge of the then embryonic computer business's foray into the technical/production side of the multibillion-dollar music and audio industry: the Synclavier Digital Audio System. It was unexpected—a quirky but magical coincidence. (BTW, Syd became a Buddhist monk and is now living in France, I believe!) After one day spent at their very-early-stage company headquarters, I became completely convinced that this new digital technology would revolutionize the very industry I had grown up in. It felt as if there was a possibility for me to kill five birds with one stone (politically correct version: to feed five birds with one feeder):

1. Generate some revenue for me and my young family without having to rely solely on the fickle fame and fortune of the crazy music biz.
2. Stay in, around, and near my beloved, fickle, crazy music biz.
3. Generate revenue by introducing my existing network of artists and companies to this new technology.
4. Have access to this amazing wizardry for my own music production projects.
5. Have influence on the evolution of this technology by helping the company understand exactly how people like me would use it in the field.

To make a long story shorter, I was, at first, the regional Northeast distributor for NED. Then I started a company that housed the demo of the Synclavier in New York City and sold the concept as well as the systems (which cost several hundred thousand dollars at that point) to top figures in the music and film/TV postproduction communities.

After several years, NED bought out my company in a stock swap, gave me a healthy salary and incentives, and I became their world-wide director of sales, traveling far and wide to pitch, cultivate, and close artists such as Sting, Stevie Wonder, Mark Knopfler, Michael Jackson, Pat Metheny, Frank Zappa, and Paul Simon, and post-production companies such as Lucasfilm and many others. NED grew quickly. It was a very creative time and lots and lots of fun too. It was also hard work.

Then several conditions shifted, for the company and for me personally:

1. I felt that the company would inevitably hit a bump as the technology became more available, computer hardware became dramatically less expensive, and the knockoffs began to abound.
2. I felt that I was spending too much of my time on the business (livelihood) side and too little on my creative side.
3. I also experienced, at this transformative time, the end of my life as I knew it. Starting in 1987 and running through 1988, CTR passed away, my father and his second wife died by suicide together after his long and painful bout with Parkinson's disease, and my marriage to Janice ended painfully.

It was not a particularly happy time for me, and my livelihood had to be reinvented yet again.

It's kind of cathartic and exhilarating in a way to relate this narrative that covers seven years or so of my life on earth. But the main reason I'm including this story is that it was a tremendous learning experience for me. When I once again found myself at a professional crossroads, I did so armed with hard-earned insights. Let's unpack some of these:

1. When you spontaneously encounter a high-energy and auspicious situation, pay extra-close attention to every aspect of it.

Be prepared to scan your feelings, contemplate, assess, and act incisively when it feels appropriate.

2. If, after meeting an opportunity, feeling the energy, and carefully deliberating, you decide to move forward with a business adventure, lean in and commit. Retreat is occasionally mandated, but many of us retreat too soon, overwhelmed by doubt, uncertainty, and a lack of familiarity with the terrain.

3. If the opportunity is in alignment with your current aspiration, once you're committed, create a strategy—an overview of how you intend to be successful in this venture.

4. Once your strategy is clear, it's time to create a tactical plan. It costs nothing to plan (on paper), and a good plan can illuminate the lay of the land, potential obstacles going forward, and clarify all the elements you'll need to pull together to be successful.

   While we're on the subject, we should distinguish between a general plan (an overall strategy), an operating plan (a big-picture view of content and product development, personnel requirements, revenue and expense models, timelines, etc.), and a full-on business plan (an offering for when you need to court investors for your company).

   You should not assume that you know how to construct this third kind of document. You may need professional guidance; writing a business plan is a deep dive beyond the parameters of this book.

   In any case, the first of these is mostly the one we're talking about here.

5. Always have at least one or two trusted advisers ready to give you feedback, and listen to their advice. If you have chosen the right mentors, it's likely that they will have covered similar terrain in their own business lives and so their counsel can be invaluable. They can save you precious time, energy, and money.

6. Be aware of your own habitual patterns moving forward. If you tend to be too abrupt and demanding, that will eventually undermine your team. If you're too sweet and need too much approval, your office will turn into a daycare center.

7. Choose your team wisely.

8. Include checkpoints in your business plan—landmarks for gauging if you're on target. If you don't meet those checkpoints, don't rationalize them away.

9. Be mindful of your cash flow. Good businesses can fail, just as they start to succeed, for lack of cash.

10. As much as possible, don't take your home to work and don't take your work home.

11. Evaluate and recalibrate your plan as you go.

Now we'll see if we can't interpolate our threefold-logic framework into this discussion, so we can all benefit from my personal journey. For business purposes, though, we'll be reframing "ground, path, and fruition" as "vision, plan, and execution." Here's a simple example:

Vision: To bring a truly innovative and game-changing product to the multibillion-dollar professional music/audio marketplace.

Plan: I will utilize my expertise in the industry to help create opportunities and methods for demonstrating the desirability of this revolutionary equipment. I will create sales channels for connecting with potential customers; I will train and guide a superior sales force in presentation, cultivation, and closing skills. I will lead the process myself whenever required.

Execution: We did exactly what we set out to do, achieving and surpassing all goals as we went. Sales went from $200,000 to $25 million in five years. Personally I fed all five birds (as previously mentioned) with one feeder.

NED did go belly-up a few years later, as the knockoffs pushed them out of the game. Now you can get much of the functionality of a Synclavier Digital Audio System, which sold for $250,000 and upward, in Garage Band for free with your new laptop. Impermanence, impermanence . . .

Let's go to your workbook.

11. Vision, Plan, Execution

1. Write about a business venture you were or are currently involved in. (If the project is current, just put these questions into present tense).
2. What was your aspiration getting into this project?
3. Did you create a plan? How did you conceive your threefold logic for this project? How did it pan out?
4. Did you have sufficient funding? How was your cash flow?
5. Did you find the right people to work with?
6. Did you have good advisers?
7. Did you track your plan in real time? With timelines and checkpoints?
8. How did your own habitual patterns play into the situation? Did you self-assess as you went?
9. How did your work life and your home life overlap? Was it a healthy situation for you and your family?

Part III Some Simple Business Principles

IN PART 3 we're going to have a look at several very straightforward business principles. We're going to talk about our ground in business as confidence, simplicity, and authenticity.

Periodically we can check in with these basic principles and reset when necessary. Even if you're an experienced professional, when you feel that your game is off, it can be so helpful to go back to basics in order to realign and get back on track. If we use the analogy of tennis, this would be like going back to our footwork; sometimes it's good to put your racquet down for a while and just get your footwork straightened out. *Then* you can work on your swing—no balls yet, just your basic swing and motion. *Then* you can work with a principle such as keeping your eye on the ball.

Working on our metaphoric tennis game that way is so similar to mindfulness meditation—just going back to our basic attitude, our basic stance, and our basic swing. Keeping our eye on the ball *is* shamatha, or one-pointed concentration.

Sometimes we can find the solutions to complex problems by tuning in to simplicity.

10 Never Negotiate against Yourself

Because of our understandable efforts to be bigger, better, smarter, stronger, richer, or more attractive, we are shadowed by a nagging sense of weariness and self-doubt.

—MARK EPSTEIN, *Advice Not Given: A Guide to Getting Over Yourself*

IN BUSINESS, and in life in general, there may be people rooting for you to fail, for you to falter, for you to doubt yourself, for you not to trust yourself—don't be one of those people!

Penetrating appraisal of your own strengths and weaknesses is an important key to success and even to being a great person, but that's completely different from working or negotiating against yourself. There's no need to program failure into your OS to avoid facing a challenge! If you're going to fail, fail honestly and learn your lessons.

Sometimes our habit of defeating ourselves before the battle has even begun may feel as if it comes from a fear of failure, but it also may come from a fear of success. CTR called this *poverty mentality*. Instead of coming from a place of inherent richness and courage, we lead with a feeling that failure is inevitable. And then, of course, our projection becomes a self-fulfilling prophecy.

For many of us, when we start to practice mindfulness meditation, we notice sooner or later that a large piece of our mental chatter is colored by harsh self-criticism. Such thoughts may seem to be embedded in the very fabric of our minds. Our story lines might even tell us that, among our other failings, we're not even good at meditation. We can't even follow two breaths in a row without our attention wandering! For some of us, it's difficult to get over this hurdle, lighten up, and give ourselves an honest chance at this new practice.

What's missing in poverty mentality is kindness and compassion toward ourselves. If we have deeply embedded habits of being too harsh and unfriendly toward ourselves, it can be very challenging to practice mindfulness. We simply run out of patience, energy, and initiative. We "gas out" on our practice.

In a situation such as this, it can be enormously helpful to pause in our perhaps too-intense drive to be perfectly aware and present, and simply contemplate kindness and gentleness toward ourselves—and toward others, while we're at it. It can be very difficult to generate kindness and compassion toward others if we can't find that feeling within ourselves first.

Metta, or loving-kindness (*maitri* in Sanskrit), is a meditation practice that, like mindfulness, goes all the way back twenty-five hundred years to the Buddha's original teachings. Metta is a great practice in all cases, but it can be especially helpful if we find that our approach to mindfulness is too tight and demanding.

Metta Meditation

Take ten minutes or so and do this practice right now, or bookmark it and try it on your own time and at your own pace later. A fuller description of the practice can be found in appendix 1.

You can begin your metta practice as if you were starting a mindfulness session: cross-legged on a cushion on the floor, or upright on a chair, ideally with strong posture and without leaning against the back of the chair or the wall. It's a good idea to first start with a short session of your mindfulness of breath practice, in order to get settled, center yourself, and gather your focus and attention.

Then follow this simple outline (take ten minutes or so):

1. Think about somebody you love and send them the following four wishes:

> May you be safe.
> May you be healthy.
> May you be happy.
> May you be at ease.

You can either repeat these phrases (silently to yourself) or take turns with each phrase and contemplate its meaning while thinking about the person you love. What would bring them greater security, happiness, well-being, and peace? Just think about that.

2. Now offer the four wishes to yourself.

3. Now offer the four wishes to somebody you don't know very well, or at all.

4. Finally, offer the four wishes to somebody who is annoying, hostile, irritating, difficult, or challenging.

5. See what comes up for you in each case, and simply do your best to open your heart and offer the people (let's include animals and all kinds of beings while we're at it) your sincere good wishes for their health and happiness.

After you finish your loving-kindness meditation, you can simply return to your mindfulness meditation for a few minutes to allow your mind to rest and be still. Your project of loving everybody and telling the truth can simply relax and dissolve for a few moments.

You may find that certain parts of the metta practice go very smoothly and others are more challenging. The feeling may change each time you do the practice (or any practice!); the process and outcome may feel different. That is ideal. We're not trying to create some predictable state of mind and then freeze-dry it for eternity. The mind doesn't work that way at all.

You're simply working with your mind and heart as they are, starting fresh every time you sit down to practice. The key is to clearly and steadily apply the method of the practice you're doing. You may have occasional epiphanies, but it's much more often the case that you're gradually cultivating the quality you're working with (mindfulness, compassion, wisdom, insight, confidence, etc.) and creating the foundation for those qualities to manifest more frequently in your everyday life.

OK, so now that we're softened up, and ready to be kinder to ourselves and others, let's return to the issue of never negotiating against yourself.

I owe the particular message of this chapter to my lifelong attorney, dear friend, and publishing partner Judith Berger.

Judy came into my career early on. Warner Bros. Records was about to release the Maria Muldaur album that featured "Midnight at the Oasis" along with another song I'd written.

It turned out that I had to actually publish those songs in order to collect my portion of the royalties. I had literally no experience and no idea what that even meant, and an executive at Warner Bros., Mary Martin, was kind enough to introduce me to her friend—attorney and publishing specialist Judy Berger.

We met for lunch at a restaurant in Manhattan. I was so green at the time that it never even occurred to me that a fancy Manhattan restaurant might have a dress code—I had to wear a jacket they kept in the closet for knuckleheads like me. (Oops . . . there I go; I already forgot my loving-kindness toward myself! I mean for *neophytes* like me. ☺)

For years after that, Judy negotiated various publishing deals, recording contracts, and film and TV music contracts for me. Often, while negotiating, I would try to look at the deal from the other person's point of view—for instance, I'd think about what kind of budget and expectation they might have. Of course, within limits, this can be a reasonable and helpful thing to do. In my case, even though I was trying to avoid overshooting the mark and messing up the deal, sometimes I was actually undermining my own confidence and sense of self-worth.

And Judy would simply say to me, pretty much every time, "David, don't negotiate against yourself!"

Over the years it occurred to me that this approach could also have a wider, more inclusive meaning. When we lack confidence, for whatever reason, we can easily underestimate our own value and the value of whatever it is that we're presenting as our offering.

That's not to say that we shouldn't be able to come up with a realistic assessment of our offering's current value. Negotiation really is an art. And in some sense, we're almost always in a process of negotiation—even our intimate relationships have an ongoing theme of negotiation.

Overcome poverty mentality.

Our business can only succeed to the level of success we'll allow in our life. We experience poverty mentality when we can't access our own internal sense of richness and worthiness.

Please go to your workbook.

12. Negotiation

1. Self-assess your level of confidence in the quality and value of your offering. (Remember, here we're talking about bringing your offering to the commercial marketplace.)
2. What are some ways in which you might occasionally

undermine the value of your offering and therefore go into a negotiation low on confidence and self-esteem—and thereby weaken your valuation before you've even started to talk?

3. Can you also identify times in which you overestimated your value, came across as too arrogant, and lost what could have been a valuable opportunity? Write down any you can think of.

4. How would you describe your negotiating skills—strong? weak? skilled? disorganized? Discuss.

Of course, no matter how skilled a negotiator you might be, sometimes it can still be better to have an attorney, business partner, or manager handle this side of your business for you. Bringing in a surrogate can allow you to keep your relationship with the client less adversarial, or it might give you the opportunity to play "good cop, bad cop"—a time-honored negotiation strategy. (Of course, in that scenario you would be the good cop!)

11 Keep It Simple and User Friendly

That's been one of my mantras—focus and simplicity. Simple can be harder than complex; you have to work hard to get your thinking clean to make it simple.

—STEVE JOBS

IF YOU'RE ANYTHING like me, you don't enjoy reading manuals and you get easily frustrated using new tools—you just want the damn things to work.

I realize that a small percentage of you roll the other way and enjoy taking things apart and putting them back together. As a boy in Tibet, the Dalai Lama was famous for disassembling and reassembling Swiss watches. There's a certain kind of mind that delights in that kind of thing, and it's usually marked by tremendous patience.

As for me, my personal tech hero is Steve Jobs; his whole drive toward stylish, user-friendly tools for humans was clearly what made Apple unique and so successful. I watch with some amusement how the culture he created still tries to follow this trend, yet at times seems to veer back into the arcane and feature-laden rabbit hole that technology can so easily take us down.

Of course, sometimes we have to strike a balance. Technical software, like the music production software we use in my industry, has to have a certain level of sophistication or it will sacrifice depth of functionality. To really see both sides of this issue, we need to imagine an x–y grid with depth of function on one axis and ease of engagement on the other.

When we study and teach Buddhism, for example, there's often a tension between expressing the subtlety and profundity of the deeper teachings, and communicating in a straightforward and simple way. Many Buddhist teachers (and many other kinds of communicators) have leaned either toward going wide or going deep. The best can do both and strike a balance, but it's not easy.

If we examine our own patterns, we might see that we lean either toward depth of expression on the one hand or accessibility on the other. It can be helpful to assess periodically and tweak these tendencies in order to achieve balance. It's also totally fine for some of us to lean more toward one or the other of these modalities. Most good companies have both aspects represented; we just need to make sure we have coworkers or systems in place to provide balance. Similarly, in a healthy company or system, there will be a balance between the generation of pure content and the assessment of who out there in the real world might possibly be interested in what's being offered—a balance between content and marketing.

In any case, learning to express ourselves succinctly and precisely can be extremely valuable. In the entertainment world (as well as in other entrepreneurial environments) there's something we call an "elevator pitch."

The premise is that the person you're making your pitch to—possibly somebody who could empower, support, or finance your project—is on an elevator with you. You have an extremely limited time to introduce your idea and make a compelling case for the other person to want to follow up with you about it—usually thirty seconds or twenty-five words, max! If you're too vague or long-winded, your person gets off the elevator at their floor and that unique opportunity may be gone forever. And, of course, you also have to make your case without being too pushy or speedy.

Here's a fictional example of what would be one of the greatest elevator pitches of all time: Albert Einstein gets on the elevator with the head of the nuclear physics department at Columbia University,

makes eye contact, pauses for a moment, and then says, "E = MC². "
Einstein hands the department head his card, bows slightly, and gets
off the elevator at his floor, never looking back.

Here are a few other whimsical pitches to convey the idea:

- *Star Wars*: a sci-fi, samurai-ish, good-versus-evil galactic space epic.
- iPhone: a completely integrated digital communication device you can put in your pocket.
- Pizza: a round, flat piece of bread with a delicious variety of toppings—you can cut it into slices and walk out eating one. Was once Italian.

Let's go to your workbook.

13. Elevator Pitches

1. Construct an elevator pitch for a creative project you're contemplating.
2. Now create an elevator pitch for a business venture you're either launching or contemplating.
3. How would you succinctly and precisely describe your current livelihood? Primary relationship? Strengths? Weaknesses? Spiritual practice? Aspirations?

The purpose of these exercises is to simplify, to shed pounds and pounds of extra baggage, while still being careful not to lose meaning and subtlety. Can we communicate succinctly, precisely, and compellingly without dumbing down or oversimplifying our message? It's very challenging to achieve this kind of communication but can be very effective and very powerful.

It's almost like poetry—like a haiku. We don't always have to say everything we think and pull people into our inner ramblings. Keep it simple and user friendly. When it's time for a deeper dive, we're ready with our scuba gear—two sets, one for us and one for our guest.

12 Put a Ring on It

Protecting Your Intellectual Property

Intellectual property is the oil of the twenty-first century.
—MARK GETTY, cofounder of Getty Images

So, YOU'VE CREATED your offering and you're bringing it to the marketplace. This is a great time to explore one aspect of the relationship between creativity and making a buck.

When we create a unique set of ideas—or a particular formulation of words, images, sounds (such as a movie or video), etc.—it's called *intellectual property* (IP), at least while this concept lasts and is still protected by law. I often recommend it as one of the best possible kinds of property to own, requiring the least maintenance while delivering a potentially expansive yield.

The two ways to protect intellectual property are by adding a copyright notice (with date) to the work (and ultimately registering it with the government) or patenting certain ideas, such as paper clips or Scotch tape (and also registering with the government). In either case, obviously somebody else can simply ignore your claim to have created something unique, and you'll have to go to court to defend your ownership of that concept, notion, or particular arrangement. But in theory, a copyright or patent means that anytime someone uses your idea—for instance, by putting your song in a commercial—they have to pay you for the right to use it.

Songs are an especially lovely type of IP. Every time your song is played on the radio, TV, and elsewhere, you get paid. It's kind of miraculous. You can get fired from your job, deplete all your savings, and be ready to sell your house and car, and then you walk to the mailbox and out drops a nice fat check for a song you wrote thirty years earlier. It's like Monopoly money; it barely feels real—but it is!

When "Midnight at the Oasis" was a big radio hit, I remember getting a check in the mail and going right down to the car dealership and buying a brand-new Toyota Corona with cash. I was a little conservative and not used to that kind of return on investment, so I didn't buy a Ferrari . . . but you can bet that others did.

My old friend and talented songwriter Greg Prestopino called me up a while back with a dilemma. He had cowritten a hit song titled "Break My Stride," which had already made him a nice chunk of change. Now they wanted to license it for a TV commercial for adult/geriatric diapers. (Funny idea, no?) He was having a conflict about letting his song be used in that context, but he got over it when he contemplated, with my encouragement, the advance being offered for that usage.

Intellectual property can be just the best kind of cash cow and a gift that keeps on giving—while it lasts.

I'm adding "while it lasts" to the definition of IP because some schools of thought, especially in the digital era, advocate eliminating the notion of intellectual property and making all data-based info part of the public domain (sometimes also called *crowdsourced*). The notion is that data is now so easy to move around, add to, rearrange, and distribute that the concept of intellectual property might just dissolve into the ether.

Records, music, video, film, software, etc., are all now so much easier to simply pass along in a digital format to anybody who wants them, without paying for the work that went into making them— your creative work! So far, entertainment industries have adapted to changing times (to some extent) with paid downloads and subscription services, but the writing might be on the wall—or more correctly, in the cloud.

If our creativity needs the body and the physical world to manifest something tangible—cooking, building, designing clothing and buildings, running a service-based business, physical training, governing—that might be more trackable than something more abstract such as IP. However, even there, if you're a futurist like I am, there are projections about all that, ranging from downloadable human identity to programmable matter. But that will remain a wormhole for another occasion!

If you want to make a side trip and speculate about our possible future in these areas, a few seminal books are *The Future* by Al Gore, *The Singularity Is Near* by Ray Kurzweil, and *The Future of Humanity* by Michio Kaku: davidnichtern.com/future

It might be the case that we can't even conceptualize the shape of commodity, service, and technology even fifty years from now. But in the meantime, maintaining IP rights is still one of the best ways to link our creativity with making a buck. So we should be strongly aware of how IP can generate revenue and how delicate it can be, and we should consider keeping up with all parameters of IP as that situation evolves.

Let's go to your workbook.

14. Intellectual Property

1. Do you have any ideas that inherently, just by themselves, might potentially have value? Something that maybe nobody has thought of yet? Or maybe something that meets an existing need but is a cut above any other solution to date? The classic example is "a better mousetrap." Can you think of any kind of better mousetrap?

2. If so, do you know how to protect your idea? How to create a copyright or apply for a patent?

3. How might you expand an existing business to include some kind of IP? For example, a yoga studio that could be selling online classes or teacher trainings, or a music store that could be selling instructional videos?

13 Authenticity and Integrity

Success doesn't count unless you earn it fair and square.

—MICHELLE OBAMA

WHATEVER WE'RE TRYING to present to others—whatever message or product we're trying to impart, for fun, profit, charity, or whatever other reasons we might have—we should be the 3D poster child for that message, from our outer appearance, to our behavior, to our speech, all the way through to the marrow of our bones.

At the end of the day, our brand will be a mirror image of who we are—and the more authentic we are, the better. To some extent we live in a culture that sometimes rewards image, bluster, and fabrication, but I recommend that we each take a warrior's leap right over that junk pile and learn how to be, manifest, and radiate what we Buddhists call *authentic presence.*

I think we can see that, for the most part, our heroes and role models are unique, original, inspired, and authentic.

Authenticity is an important thread in this book. Here we're not presenting success and thriving as a clever fabrication that we need to create and maintain but as a genuine and organic outflow of our truest nature.

Don't sell something you don't like, don't create due to convenience or trends, don't try to con and swindle people to get ahead. If this wisdom is old school and feels dated, I can live with that.

REMEMBER INTEGRITY?

As I'm writing this book, it feels as if we're living in a time when the notion of integrity has been completely usurped and abandoned.

In "The Sadhana of Mahamudra," Chögyam Trungpa Rinpoche wrote,

> This is the darkest hour of the dark ages. Disease, famine and warfare are raging like the fierce north wind. The Buddha's teaching has waned in strength. The various schools of the sangha are fighting amongst themselves with sectarian bitterness; and although the Buddha's teaching was perfectly expounded and there have been many reliable teachings since then from other great gurus, yet they pursue intellectual speculations. The sacred mantra has strayed into Bön and the yogis of tantra are losing the insight of meditation. They spend their whole time going through villages and performing little ceremonies for material gain.

CTR wrote this just before he came to the West. At the time, Tibet had been completely overrun by the Chinese invasion. The reason I'm including it here is that, even though his words clearly come from a spiritual practice, he's really talking about the condition of our world and how greed, anxiety, and blind materialism can overwhelm and undermine our personal sense of decency, wholesomeness, and authenticity. When CTR came to the West I think he felt that this kind of description applied, in its own way, to our modern materialistic culture.

There has been an almost complete disconnect between honesty, integrity, compassion, and ethical conduct in many of our institutions and their operating systems. In the United States, outright lying and manipulation, always part of the political system, have come to completely dominate it, at least for the moment, as of this writing.

Right now, people are really freaking out; they're afraid of each other, their own shadows, the truth—it's truly starting to feel like the dark ages spoken of in so many spiritual traditions. Even in popular mythology such as *Star Wars,* the dark side *is powerful.*

Buddhist teachings and other wisdom traditions advocate ethics and integrity. They proclaim the basic goodness of all beings and the possibility of enlightened society, even in the face of great danger and intimidation. As a student and teacher in this tradition, I constantly scrutinize my own motivation, intention, and personal discipline, especially before teaching a program or writing a book like this.

This brings us back to authenticity: as a teacher or leader, you either walk it like you talk it or you become the worst kind of phony bullshit artist.

So we're closing part 3 with an inspirational suggestion—*be authentic.* If you operate with integrity, you'll never really fail in your journey. Every situation will be a learning situation. For a warrior, the world is a perfect mirror.

In parts 4, 5, and 6, we're going to look at how we can personally cultivate the qualities that will help us achieve spiritual and temporal excellence. Before doing so, let's visit your workbook for a moment.

15. Review Your Progress

1. Pick out any themes or issues that have emerged for you so far. What are the highlights either in the presentation or in your own responses? What topics would you like to revisit at some point in the future and explore more deeply?

Part IV Interpersonal Skills
and Ethical Conduct

IN PART 4 we're going to shift our focus to the cultivation of interpersonal skills—how to conduct ourselves in an uplifted, authentic, responsible way—in relation to our partners, colleagues, employees, and bosses. We're taking the view that ethical conduct is the foundation of genuine success in life *and* in business.

14 Don't Blame, Don't Make Excuses, Don't Whine

Take off your bedroom slippers, put on your marching shoes. Shake it off. Stop complaining. Stop grumbling. Stop crying. We are going to press on. We've got work to do.

—PRESIDENT BARACK OBAMA

IN ALL HONESTY, I'm still working on this one. It's so difficult to stop blaming others, stop making excuses, and stop whining. It's almost a knee-jerk reaction when the going gets tough. But in order to fully manifest our vision, aspiration, and intention in this very lifetime, we have to look at ourselves and self-assess.

Good leaders take responsibility. If you find that you're constantly pointing out the shortcomings of others, turn the mirror around so it's facing you.

Accountability is a matter of ethics, genuine pride, and personal authenticity. Whether anyone or no one or the whole world is watching, our personal conduct should be impeccable if we want to realize our fullest potential in business, in life, in relationships, and as a leader and creative force in this world.

Many traditions, including Buddhism, shamanism, the ancient samurai culture of Japan, the knight tradition of Europe, the medical profession, and more, have a code of conduct that's clearly identified and often accompanied by a variety of oaths and commitments. If we look at the samurai code of *bushido*, for example, we see that it was structured around eight virtues: righteousness, heroic courage, benevolence, respect, integrity, honor, duty, and self-control.

Why are we talking about all this in a contemporary business context? Because in business an accomplished leader should be free from jealousy, pettiness, complaint, and small-mindedness.

When we blame, make excuses, or whine, we inevitably weaken our personal power and potency in whatever situation we find ourselves. Our energy dribbles out as if from a leaky balloon and soon we become like a chicken who can't fly and just wanders around the barnyard squawking and waiting for death to come.

When we become fully accountable, take responsibility, and are mindful of our thoughts and speech, we gather power and strengthen our innate capacity to work with even difficult and challenging situations. We become like an eagle or the *garuda* from Indian mythology, who flies without ever needing to land. We can go beyond conventional reference points of success and failure, continuously refreshing our energy by transforming even challenging situations from obstacles into opportunities.

From a warrior's point of view, living in the challenge is more valuable than any kind of result or endgame scenario we could envision, even one with a fantastic outcome. This kind of attitude allows us to finally peel away the layers of resentment, complaint, and poverty mentality that inevitably cause us to doubt ourselves and others and to repeat the same mistakes over and over again—and move forward and upward in manifesting our vision.

Please go to your workbook.

📖 16. Becoming Accountable

1. Give an accurate assessment of your tendency to blame others
   and create an atmosphere of obstacle and complaint in your

work life. You can do this with your personal and family relationships too, if you feel extra ambitious.

2. Can you envision a process through which you could shift your patterns in this area toward accountability, responsibility, and fearless leadership? How might you change these patterns? What would it take to move in that direction for you?

3. Work through a specific example in which you defaulted in your leadership role at work and gave in to the ongoing temptation to generate an atmosphere of complaint, anxiety, and recrimination.

4. How would you describe the qualities of leadership that you value?

5. Create your own warrior code of personal conduct and ethics, one you view as admirable and worthy of cultivating. Make a list of as many aspects for this code as you wish, with perhaps a brief commentary on each.

6. Now take your own code and note where you feel your strong points and weak points are as of now. How can you stabilize your strengths and strengthen your weaknesses for each point? Be fearless and honest.

Remember—honest self-assessment is the backbone of everything we're talking about in this book. In Buddhism we have a slogan:

Of the two witnesses, take the principal one.

Rather than trying to impress, to gain approval, or to accommodate—rather than basing our actions on how we think others see us—we're willing to keep our own counsel as to what to cultivate and what to avoid.

15 Everybody Wants to Be Appreciated. Appreciate Them!

Everyone responds to kindness.
—RICHARD GERE

COMPOSING AND PRODUCING music has been my principal livelihood for most of my adult life. What a challenging way to pay the bills! It really takes dedication and effort to make a living as a musician year after year. So whenever I see a person on the subway playing a violin or alto sax, I offer an inner bow to that brave warrior and drop at least a buck (talk about "making a buck"!) or more into their hat or case.

Everybody wants to be appreciated for their contribution; everybody deserves some kind of praise and support for their efforts. We're not talking about effusive, unearned praise with some kind of sugar coating and happy face attached. We're talking about appreciating those people who work with us and work for us.

As a composer and musician, I've had many bosses over many years. Some have been exceptional and generous, some reasonable, some difficult, and some outright abusive.

It's important to note that the quality of a leader or artist's work isn't necessarily dependent on their qualities as a human being. In fact, sometimes there seems to be an inverse proportion between the quality of an artist's work and their benevolence and good qualities as an employer—or as a human being. This paradigm can hold true for many famous business and government leaders as well.

But the quality of an artist or businessperson's work is also *not dependent* on them being a slave driver, a sociopathic narcissist, or a nasty person. We'll be talking about creativity in its own right later on in our discussion. All we're saying here is that being wildly creative and being a good employer or friend each have their own independent basis, and we can be *both*.

It's fine to negotiate skillfully, to protect our interests, to have very high standards for our work and the work of others, to offer constructive criticism, to be direct and straightforward (hopefully skillfully), etc. But it's not OK to abuse our coworkers, employees, friends, lovers, family members, etc. It *is* important for us to appreciate them and praise them appropriately—to recognize their good qualities and efforts, and actually express our awareness of them in word and deed.

People are part of the animal kingdom, of course, but we bloom like flowers when we receive praise and support for our efforts.

OK . . . let's stay with our making-a-buck world for now—let's go to your workbook.

17. Move Away from Abuse and toward Appreciation

1. Write down any experiences you've had with being insufficiently appreciated—or, if you're up for it, abused—in your work world. Try to be discerning and separate out real incidences in which you were treated unfairly from incidences that might have resulted from a clash of personality, miscommunication, or shared blame. Talk about the feelings you had in those situations. Go ahead—get it out of your system.

2. Now write down any work experiences in which, in all honesty and humble acknowledgment, you were the abuser. Talk about those feelings as you now perceive them.

3. Describe your aspiration in this area, both on the receiving

end and on the giving end. You can even make amends, forgive anyone you feel you would like to forgive, and generally disencumber yourself from carrying around these kinds of negative feelings and projections. Be your own guru or shrink and work through any karma in this area. Write about it.

16 Lying, Cheating, and Stealing Aren't Good for You or Anybody Else

Ethical Conduct and the Law of Karma

If you are a liar, it's not going to work out for you.
—DUNCAN TRUSSELL, podcaster and podmaster
for the *Duncan Trussell Family Hour*

A CODE of ethical conduct is the backbone of a well-lived life. This brings us again to the notion of karma—the dance of cause and effect.

In this book we're reducing karma to its simplest possible dimension: *what we think, say, and do matters*. Buddhism teaches us that our thoughts, speech, and actions are impermanent, empty, insubstantial, and in some sense unreal—this view is called the *absolute or unconditional truth*. But Buddhism also teaches us that they matter, that they have profound impact—this view is called the *relative truth*. These two truths are inseparable; the latter is every bit as important to understand and relate to if we want to develop deep spiritual understanding.

The law of karma tells us that every thought, every word we say, and every action we take will create a ripple, like a stone tossed into a pond. Sooner or later (sometimes much later), the imprint we create will return and come home to roost. This is true for positive actions, which generate well-being and benefit for ourselves and others, and negative actions, which create pain and confusion for ourselves and others. There's no place we can go, in this universe or any other, to escape this ripple.

When we bring our understanding of karma to the business world, it translates in part to this really simple premise: Don't lie, don't cheat, and don't steal. Period. Even if we have an opportunity to land that big account, make a fortune, get a raise or promotion, create the biggest lifestyle brand on the planet, have a hit record . . . we can still strive to be ethical, straightforward, and honest.

Maintaining our ethical code doesn't mean we can't be clever, brilliant, strategic, discreet, inscrutable, tactical, etc. But there's a clear line when it comes to ethical conduct, and every time we cross it we create negative karma for ourselves and others.

Life is like a giant credit card. If we don't pay our karmic debts as we create them, they will come back to us later—with interest. This isn't moralizing—it's how the world works, with or without us in it. You break it, you pay for it!

When we look at the notion of ethical conduct, there are really two dimensions to explore. The first and perhaps most obvious aspect is our outer expression—how we treat others. It can be fairly straightforward to simply create and honor a particular code, one that includes being honest, fair, and reliable. If we're in a leadership position, we can always lead by example.

The second and perhaps more subtle aspect is an inner process—how we hold ourselves accountable to the narrative we create around who we are and what we're doing. We'll have more to say about self-deception in chapter 21, but here let's focus on remembering that it's always possible that we think we're being ethical in our dealings with people while our internal wiring in this area might be frayed or tangled.

Sometimes all can appear dignified and righteous on the surface, but there's mold underneath. Recently we've seen leaders in the spiritual, political, business, and entertainment communities who have the appearance of propriety but underneath there's subterfuge, manipulation, and abuse of power and authority. We've also seen situations in which the perpetrator himself (or herself) seems genuinely unaware of their own dark side and its expression, even in the face of their proclamation of ethical conduct.

As human beings, part of our makeup can be hidden even from ourselves. The tells for this kind of distortion are when we justify, resent, rationalize, and ignore and/or repress certain provocative realizations concerning our integrity that might be lurking in the shadows of our own mind. Discovering this obfuscation is an important part of the spiritual journey. There are always deeper and deeper levels of scrutiny and honesty that can uncover our habitual patterns at subtler and subtler levels.

Accordingly, we can and should contemplate if and when we have caused harm to others and be willing to apologize, clean up any mess we made, and create a clear and strong intention to not repeat the same pattern in the future. We all have made mistakes, and in all likelihood we'll make more in the future. But we can create a strong intention to dig deeper, acknowledge any unskillful and self-centered actions, and purify our internal and external ethical eco-systems. This kind of evaluation is an important aspect of leadership and personal evolution.

A clear and tangible indicator of our outer ethical direction is simply noticing the ripples of our interpersonal relationships in our business community. If we pay attention as situations unfold, rather than spacing out and being surprised by the outcome, I think we can see how our words and actions begin to create a weather system in our work and home environment. It can be helpful to course correct as the weather system evolves rather than waiting to experience the full impact of the hurricane winds, tsunamis, and flooding that can be the outcome of seemingly insignificant words and actions. The full consequence could be loss of key employees or clients, but an early warning system might allow us to shift the energy before it comes to that.

A standard cliché is that we'll meet the same people on our way down as we did on our way up, so we might want to think twice about mistreating people when we're moving toward success. However, I don't regard business as charity. Of course we want to support our employees, colleagues, even bosses in their journey through life, but I don't believe that includes carrying those who aren't being productive and accountable. Family businesses are notorious for this kind of enabling, and some businesses, at times, are run as if the staff is like a family. This can create a fun and hearty atmosphere at work, but it can also create dysfunction and all kinds of unwholesome outcomes.

We shouldn't see our employees, associates, and competitors as enemies to be crushed, nor should we create a false and syrupy atmosphere of superficial generosity and unsustainable benevolence. This approach is yet another expression of taking the Middle Way.

The outcome of establishing ethical conduct can be that we hold the same high standards for those we work for, those we work with, and those who work for us as we do for ourselves—creating a warm but still precise atmosphere. If we lead by example, it's reasonable to invite those above and below us in the food chain to follow suit. Ethical conduct sets an invisible bar for others to follow.

Let's go to your workbook.

18. Lying, Cheating, and Stealing

1. How would you rate your level of ethical conduct at work? You can give a fair and balanced account. Again, nobody but you ever has to read these comments!
2. Can you think of specific incidents where your conduct fell short of your own ideals? How did it make you feel? Did you just move on, or did you exert some effort to make amends with others who may have experienced negative impact from your actions?

3. Can you think of times when you have bent your own code of ethical conduct and it felt OK, even kind of cool, as if you were getting away with something and the notion of accountability seemed irrelevant? This can be particularly interesting to explore.

17 Be Merciful to Others

You can't tell somebody something if they don't have a place to put it. —Uncle Irv

T HRIVING CAN *never* be based on fear and aggression. Even if aspects of our current social and political reality are spiraling downward, we can act appropriately and lift them back up.

One of the traditional lojong slogans is this:

Don't bring things to a painful point.

In a nutshell, this slogan goes hand in hand with the notion of taking responsibility, not putting blame on others, and, as previously expressed here, appreciating others' efforts and contribution. Naturally there will be times when somebody we work with or who works for us will make, gods forbid, a mistake. We should be able to recognize such a thing, because it will possibly remind us of the four hundred million mistakes we ourselves have already made. Bringing things to a painful point is like kicking somebody when they're already down—it's not necessary or productive. We can simply give a clear assessment, together with guidelines for how to proceed, and perhaps some consequences and boundaries for similar situations should they arise in the future.

It's important to be able to provide leadership, accurate and constructive direction, and guidance at work, but we can—and should—mix in the quality of mercy and forgiveness along with sharp, clear, penetrating insight and feedback. Not bringing things to a painful point doesn't mean that we try to work around challenging situations or that we try to avoid difficult conversations. We can be direct and to the point at work, but we can be skillful and diplomatic at the same time. Even if we have to fire somebody, we can be clear and honest—we don't have to be merciless and abusive.

When we do need to have a difficult conversation with a fellow employee, boss, or subordinate, we should be mindful of choosing the right time and place for the meeting, and we should be aware of who else should or should not be present—and the possible ripple effect of our communication. Our office or studio can be a petri dish for gossip, backstabbing, rumors, and insinuations, and we should try not to feed those gnarly little gremlins.

One way to avoid bringing things to a painful point is to allow release along the way, so we don't end up exploding at somebody while half the office watches with their mouths open, wondering who will be next. In many professional situations, regular formal reviews are part of the operating system, and that's probably a healthy method for avoiding the buildup of emotions and long-held personal or professional issues.

We're talking about dialing down abuse and self-righteousness in the workplace. If we communicate skillfully as the situation evolves, the chances of dramatic eruptions will be minimized. These are obviously high standards for the workplace, but we can strive for them if we want to be truly successful.

The lojong slogans are very precise and pithy. Traditionally, teachers along the way have offered commentary on these slogans, to flesh them out a bit and help us tune in to their essence.

Judy Lief, senior Buddhist teacher and editor of many of CTR's books, offered a commentary on this particular slogan in *Tricycle* magazine. Here's an excerpt:

> According to this slogan, instead of pouncing on people's weaknesses and vulnerabilities, we should be providing encouragement and support for their strengths. That's what we should notice and point out, not just what's wrong. The idea is that it is more skillful to encourage positive qualities than to criticize what is negative. With this approach, we are not using others to heighten our own confidence nor are we undermining other people's confidence by reminding them of their inadequacies.

Here's a link to Judy's whole commentary, called "Train Your Mind": davidnichtern.com/slogan

Reading commentaries on the lojong slogans, and on essential Buddhist teachings in general, can deepen our understanding. By giving us a variety of reference points, they can enrich our comprehension of both the meaning of the teaching and how to go about putting it to work for us in everyday life.

If you want to check this practice out further, Pema Chödrön's "Compassion Box" is a great option: davidnichtern.com/pema

Let's go to your workbook.

19. Alternatives to the Painful Point

1. Can you think of a time when you *did* bring things to a painful point with a colleague or friend?
2. Tune in to your motivation. What was it, and how did it make you feel?
3. Think about giving constructive feedback in a difficult situation without feeling the need to denigrate or even humiliate the other person. How might you create a more positive outcome for others and for the whole situation?

18 Lids and Flowers
Enlightened Hierarchy

Leadership is not domination, but the art of persuading people to
work toward a common goal.

—DANIEL GOLEMAN, *Emotional Intelligence:
Why It Can Matter More Than IQ*

AT A CRITICAL juncture in the evolution of my Buddhist community, there was some confusion about how leadership and
hierarchy could manifest in a creative and productive way.

Of course, it was the early '70s and we were all hippies—we'd
all discarded the formal, structured elements of our own society.
We were pot-smoking, acid-dropping, commune-living, free-loving
folks, rebelling against authority, protesting unjust wars, and pushing back against the established norms of our society in myriad ways.
We had discovered (or so we thought) the formula for dismantling
the existing and constricting order and creating an open and "free"
system—"turn on, tune in, and drop out."

We had heroes such as Allen Ginsberg, Wavy Gravy, Timothy
Leary, and Richard Alpert (soon to be known as Ram Dass). We
were rejecting our own spiritual traditions and exploring the mys-
teries and philosophies of the Far East and other wisdom traditions
from around the world—from Buddhism to Hinduism to Taoism to
shamanism—you name it, we were exploring it.

It was on that wave that my Tibetan teacher, Chögyam Trungpa,
surfed into the United States and gathered a bunch of us together

as students, early adopters, rabid admirers, supporters, and co-conspirators. The irony was that Trungpa Rinpoche had come from a very formal, highly structured, classical tradition. Yet somehow he managed to meet us where we were. It was an improbable but compelling alliance.

As our community grew, it was inevitable that we begin to integrate more form, more structure, to accommodate the increasing number of people who wanted to gather to study and practice this ancient wisdom tradition. Rinpoche began to create a hierarchy of teachers, administrators, translators, etc., to create a larger platform. At the time, this organization was called Vajradhatu—a Tibetan word meaning "indestructible, all-encompassing space"—a place for transmitting and learning the traditional teachings of Buddhism.

Coming from an American culture that was born from rebellion against the existing hierarchy (remember the Revolutionary War?), and that had, particularly among my generation, evolved to think of hierarchy as based on greed and power-tripping, we naturally created a (sometimes) confused and egocentric version of these structures. We had no model whatsoever for enlightened hierarchy based on wisdom, experience, vision, and mutual respect. It was like trying to produce a copy of the *Mona Lisa* without ever having seen the original painting.

In 1978, Rinpoche gave a teaching called "Hierarchy, Complaint, Gossip, and Communication in an Enlightened Society," which in my mind is, to this day, a classic memo for all of us living in the modern world. It introduced the metaphors of "lids" and "flowers," and it outlined how to create leadership structures based on wisdom and compassion rather than on power, greed, and domination. Here's an excerpt:

> As far as working with the organization, the notion of *hierarchy* is important for you to understand. . . . In our hierarchy, you have the little heads and big heads. All sorts of things are happening, but they are not regarded as lids on

pots—big lids controlling the whole pot, and smaller lids controlling smaller pots. That's wrong.

It is more like different sizes of flowers growing up. You have the smaller flowers looking up, and you have bigger flowers very tall and covering the whole area. It is an upward journey, rather than suppression, particularly. . . .

Sometimes a smaller plant grows bigger. So everybody has absolute opportunity, hundred percent opportunity, from the top to the bottom. . . . Everybody has a chance to become a small plant or a gigantic plant all along.

Here's the full transcript of CTR's talk on lids and flowers: davidnichtern.com/lids

Let's go to your workbook.

20. Enlightened Hierarchy

1. What's your understanding of hierarchy?
2. Describe several situations you're involved in that have elements of hierarchical structure. Family? Community? Society? Work?
3. How do you fit into those hierarchies? What's your role?
4. Which aspects of these hierarchies work well for you?
5. Where do you experience difficulties in your relationship to these hierarchies? What problems do you feel others are bringing to the situation? What obstacles are you yourself bringing in? Old attitudes? Feelings of resentment? Ambition?
6. How do you think you could work more productively with those problems and accompanying feelings?

Part V Personal Attitude and Cultivation

IN PART 5 we're going to migrate from the realm of inter-personal, relational principles to the realm of the intrapersonal. At the end of the day, every situation we're in—whether alone, in intimate relationships, groups, communities, companies, teams, organizations, society, etc.—reflects ourselves back to ourselves.

Sometimes it can be challenging to shift a difficult interpersonal situation. Sometimes it might seem as if we're in prison, and society is the jailer holding the key. In most circumstances we find ourselves in, there are going to be some elements that are beyond our control, certain things that aren't the way we would wish them to be.

But regardless of the situations we find ourselves in, we always have the potential for controlling our own state of mind and the attitudes and strengths we bring to bear. In fact, sometimes our own reactions can be the most imprisoning part of any given situation. They can also be the key to greater freedom. So in part 5 we're going to look at strengths we can cultivate and attitudes we can modulate to empower ourselves fully as we move toward joining our heaven and our earth.

This kind of personal cultivation is really the essence of what we're calling *spiritual practice*. In a sense, we're tuning our minds to *as it is* and activating our *up to us*. How can we increase our clarity, insight, confidence, strength, and suppleness, no matter what hand we're dealt? Strengthening these virtues is the essence of what we call *warriorship*.

19 Be Fluid and Adaptable

Impermanence Is Pervasive

Be like water, my friend.

—BRUCE LEE, who was

I LIKE TO IMAGINE Groucho Marx giving a Buddhist lecture: "Impoimanence, impoimanence, impoimanence!"

Here's a classic Groucho Marx clip, "Lydia the Tatooed Lady," if you're ready for a laugh: davidnichtern.com/groucho

It's impossible to write from a Buddhist perspective without offering a deep bow in acknowledgment of the notion and experience of impermanence. To reiterate, all phenomena brought about by causes and conditions—that is, all phenomena—are subject to impermanence. But, actually, there's nothing particularly Buddhist about impermanence. It's simply an observable and important aspect of our existence.

But what's the real impact of understanding impermanence? Why dwell on such a seemingly negative part of life? Well, we don't have to shoot the messenger—there's no good reason to get angry or depressed about the facts of life.

The real message of impermanence, stripped of metaphysical and philosophical embellishment, is that we'll be more in sync with reality if we stop grasping and fixating on places, people, youth, thoughts and emotions, concepts, opinions, and fixed goals—if we become fluid and adaptable as our life circumstances unfold and evolve.

That may be a broad stroke, but let's start by just seeing what comes up if we once again contemplate impermanence.

Contemplate Impermanence II

Again, take a comfortable seat on a cushion or on a chair and bring your attention to the topic of impermanence. It might be easiest to start with an object in the physical world around you—a flower, a tree, a building, an article of clothing. Is that object subject to impermanence? Will it stay the same over time or change? Will it ultimately decay and cease to exist in its present form?

Whenever your mind wanders from the contemplation, simply notice that and gently bring your mind back to this exact topic. See if you can penetrate beyond the obvious or clichéd perceptions and move more deeply into your exploration.

After contemplating an external object, you can move to your own body. It should be fairly easy to see that your body is impermanent—the older you get, the easier it is to see!

From there you can examine your emotions, your mental states, any part of the physical universe, any aspect of your mind or experience. You can let the contemplation lead you wherever it goes. It will be different each time. Try to really dig deep and see what you come up with.

There are at least two possible outcomes when we contemplate impermanence:

1. We can become nihilistic and depressed: What's the point?

If everything is impermanent, why bother doing anything constructive? Why compose a symphony? Why run for office? Why study? Why practice anything?

2. We can become fluid, adaptable, dynamic, and empowered in every action we take—recognizing that if we understand impermanence, our actions have inherent relevance and power that are no longer based on wishful thinking and unrealistic expectations.

The value of understanding impermanence in our work life is that we can have a vision, create a strategy, design a plan, lean in with effort, and execute our plan—and still feel open enough to change course when circumstances suggest a change is necessary.

This concept might seem so obvious. In many sports, for instance, each team gathers in the locker room at halftime, assesses the first half (by looking at the score, not just checking the vibe), and shifts their strategy appropriately. But when is it halftime in our entrepreneurial or creative venture? When do we pause, examine our results to date, and recalibrate our strategy and tactics (or the whole concept, if necessary)? Have you ever just forged ahead blindly, clinging to the existing paradigm for dear life, or just out of laziness and habit, and then floundered on the rocks of impermanence and change?

Forget business for a moment. Ignoring impermanence and change is how each of us, in our physical process, in our emotional life, in our minds, is resisting this powerful aspect of life, and when we do we create suffering—that's Buddhism 101.

The obvious but often overlooked obstacle to our acceptance of impermanence is that we may not want things to change. We might be attached to the way things are and therefore might tend to ignore or resist change—which can be unsettling and provoke anxiety. Think of your reaction to puberty, to adulthood, to crossing thirty, forty, fifty, sixty, seventy, eighty; think recession, depression, war, unemployment; think aging; think illness; think old age, dying, and death.

When we can see this impermanence-change-attachment-ignoring loop in our personal lives, it can give us the motivation we need to adapt to change fluidly in our business ventures and creative projects.

As I mentioned in the intro, lots of the advice I'm giving in this book comes from evaluating my own mistakes. I'm writing this book partly because I'm older than most of you and I'm hoping you can benefit from what I've learned the hard way.

In the 1990s I had a very successful career (creatively and financially) composing music for two daytime TV standards—*One Life to Live* and *As the World Turns*. After years of hard work composing much of the music myself and logging long hours, I managed to build an excellent team of composers, an efficient method for supervising them, and a clean and clear method for accounting for royalties accrued. After seven to eight years of mastering this operation, I felt I had some extra bandwidth and a creative need to expand into a more freestyle musical project.

It had always been my dream to own my own record and publishing company. This was based on my experience at Warner Bros. Records in the '70s, where artists had been really appreciated, creativity was cultivated, and success could be very substantial. The idea of nurturing younger artists—helping them develop their concept and creating a strategy for developing a market for them—really appealed to me, both as a financial opportunity and as part of a mentoring role that had begun to feel very natural for me. I felt I could help others, and along the way create a livelihood for myself and my family—and have lots of fun.

I could have simply continued to write for the soaps. It had turned into that most valuable of all business situations: a cash cow.

Don't forget to feed the cash cow!

But that job also was subject to impermanence. After a while, the soaps—some of which had been on the air for many decades—started to slowly give way to the newer style of women's talk shows, which had a lower budget, felt more contemporary, and had a higher profit margin. Even a cash cow gets old, sick, and dies.

If you find an immortal cash cow, let me know. Perhaps the closest thing to it is the funeral business, which is, ironically, forever youthful and totally up to date. A close second might be the wedding business, because hope springs eternal—and unlike a funeral, you can have more than one per lifetime.

In any case, I had an itch. I still get those to this day; at seventy, I'm writing my first Broadway musical. By the time you're reading this, you might recognize me as the next Andrew Lloyd Nichtern, or I may have created one of several million musicals you have never heard of and never will. The odds are stupendous against success in this arena, but I'm undaunted and don't mind being a little outrageous (see chapter 26). It's all about that itch.

However, it's unlikely that I'll sink hundreds of thousands of dollars of my own money into this venture—well, maybe tens of thousands, but that's it! If I do, you have my permission to tie me to a chair and read this entire book to me at the top of your voice.

Coming back to my sweet little independent record labels: I did have a vision, a strategy, and a plan.

We had a niche market for one label, Dharma Moon, which was bringing world and New Age–style music to the burgeoning yoga scene, as well as to related environments such as massage and general health and well-being. It also mapped to my own ongoing side career (at that time) of teaching Buddhism and meditation within that community, so it brought several of my interests together.

The concept was that this niche market would be self-sustaining (not based on hits and trends) and would provide a steady stream of revenue to support our more experimental second label: 5 Points Records. This label would be organized to develop any artists we wanted to include, ranging from world to electronica to pop.

The idea here was to simply have a hit in maybe one out of ten outings. Hits were (and still are) the currency of the music business. If one of my indie artists could be brought to the level of being ready to upsell to a major record label and be successful, serious cash would flow that could easily finance the operation of both labels.

I had already made lots of money from my one bona fide hit song ("Midnight at the Oasis"), so in a way I was hooked on the concept. It's by far the easiest and most fun way to make money I have ever experienced. As mentioned, I tell all my current entrepreneurs to make sure they understand intellectual property and build some part of their venture around that concept. There's no better feeling in business than an unexpected check just falling out of your mailbox.

So what, you ask, could possibly go wrong with this carefully crafted scheme that was built on solid previous experience, that was conceptually sound, reasonable to the extreme, and carefully executed? The problem was—and here's the point of this entire chapter—I didn't reassess, I didn't recalibrate; I wasn't fluid and I didn't allow my concept to marinate and evolve in the field of actual experience. I did not, as Bruce Lee suggested, "be like water." I was too obsessed to read the tea leaves and reevaluate the situation from a grounded business perspective.

I was smoking my own pipe dreams, if you catch my meaning. I was so attached to the way I wanted it to be that I ignored the way it actually was. Remember that those are the primary causes of suffering—attachment and ignoring. I entertained both of those two seductresses to a fault. Here were some of the mistakes I made. If you *have* to make these mistakes yourself, go right ahead, but don't say nobody warned you:

1. I financed these adventures with my own cash! As mentioned, I was making very good money from my work on the soaps, and I just kept lobbing the profits into the record labels. I don't even think I kept track of how much I was sinking into the new venture.

2. I never really looked back to look forward. I kept losing money and never recalibrated.

    My concept was actually a good one, but it was about ten years behind the times. Ten years earlier, a world or New Age record that did well would sell twenty thousand or more units. But by the time I was in the game, a reasonably successful record in that genre sold more like fifteen hundred copies.

    At the same time, the chances of developing a successful artist with hit records also probably went down by a factor of ten, and a record that might have sold twenty million copies a decade ago was lucky to sell two million. My math calculations to break even and for a success story were both off by about a thousand percent!

3. After I spent all my spare cash (which was substantial), I, like an addicted moron, borrowed money to keep going. I took out second mortgages on both my very cool downtown NYC loft and my East Hampton house. I also maxed out several credit cards to the tune of several hundred thousand dollars and kept moving them around to avoid the interest payments building up.

Oh well. A well-known joke in the record biz advises that the way to make five million is to start with ten million.

Here's something I did right: I had a rescue plan, which was to sell the loft, stop the madness (close up the record labels), and level off the nosedive with the profits from the loft. In the end that's exactly what I did. I also vowed never to repeat these same mistakes again, and I haven't.

We had some significant successes along with our failures, so our concept was not completely flawed, in the end. Another possibly unforeseen asset of the digital age is that, even though many fewer people were buying tangible goods (such as CDs), the shelf life of digital music is way longer, so I continue to generate revenue from my labels to this very day.

I realize that the business wisdom I'm talking about here is perhaps mundane compared to the Buddha's discovery of old age, sickness, and death—and our attachment to our continuously destabilizing sense of self and our ignorance as to the true nature of our existence. But I think you can see that these two situations in some sense do mirror each other. In life and in business we're better served if we include a deep understanding of impermanence and change in our assessment of a situation, and act accordingly.

So let's go to your workbook to see how fluid and adaptable you are.

 ## 21. Investigating Impermanence

1. Relate a story from your personal life in which your inability to consider impermanence and change created suffering for yourself and possibly others as well.
2. Now think of a similar situation in your business life.
3. Write briefly about your feelings regarding impermanence at the most profound level: How do you feel about aging? About your own impending death?
4. Do you have a metaphysical system in place to ward off or manage any of these raw feelings? Have you examined your beliefs carefully to see if they will still have power when you face your own demise?

5. Coming back to business, can you write a message to your-self and put it in a bottle (metaphorically speaking) to warn yourself against your own tendencies—which you have now had ample opportunity to see by looking back—and vow to be smarter going forward? They say only a fool repeats the same routines and hopes for a better outcome. Have your present wisdom mind write down some advice to your future fool mind—just for fun, in any case. ✎

Before we move on, it's worth acknowledging that impermanence is also the force that allows new life to emerge: new concepts, new relationships, new ventures. It's easy to see that decay and cessation are byproducts of this principle, but it's perhaps equally valuable to see that birth and new arisings are also expressions of impermanence. Fall and winter are expressions of impermanence—but so are spring and summer.

20 Don't Take Your Self Too Seriously
The Illusory Nature of Reality

Rodney: "So I like your title, David, but I get a little confused, because everybody has to do everything, and it actually pisses me off. You have to be the most creative person in the world, then you have to be able to sell it, then you have to be a billionaire. Let's give ourselves a goddam break!"

Colleen: "Quit swearing so much!"

Rodney: "It pisses me off!"

—RODNEY YEE AND COLLEEN SAIDMAN YEE, cofounders of Yoga
Shanti, in an interview with David Nichtern about this book

THE BUDDHIST NOTION of no-self is perhaps one of the most misunderstood aspects of this tradition; it has, at times, led to negative and even nihilistic ideas regarding what these teachings have to say about individuality. Here's a Buddhist-Jewish joke circulating on the internet that does a good job illustrating this confusion: "If there's no self, then whose arthritis is this?"

A good question—well stated. Another form of grandmother's wisdom!

It's probably more accurate to say that, from a Buddhist point of view, rather than having no self, we maintain a distorted and inaccurate notion of our self—we're actually suffering from a case of mistaken identity. We could say that our sense of identity is an illusion, but it's probably better to say that certain aspects of it are illusory:

they're not based on reality but are instead based on how we've come to believe things are or how we might wish them to be.

Who Are You?

To illustrate this point, I'm going to ask you to do a short, five-minute contemplation. Once again take a solid, seated position (either on a chair or on a cushion on the floor) and bring your attention to thinking about this simple question: Who are you?

Of course, you'll think about your name, your physical attributes, your attitudes, intentions, aspirations, experience, and so on. You'll think about your personal history, your family, your community, your society, etc. But try to penetrate all the way through, if you can, to the *essential* you. Is there anything you can describe about yourself that's solid and unchanging?

Buddhism tells us that *you* as a solid, fixed, unchanging, independent, singular entity doesn't actually exist. *You* is a relative phenomenon, subject to ongoing change and eventually to dissolution, decay, and cessation. Of course, this view deeply challenges the notion of a permanent soul; it's a very provocative description of how we exist in this world. We're encouraged to find out, for ourselves, what exactly our *self* is.

But how does this understanding affect our everyday life, our creative endeavors, our business enterprises, our relationships? It's simply a matter of noticing how much we tend to solidify our sense of self and defend it, and thereby freeze our perceptions of the world around us, of the people we live with, the people we work with, and our community and societal partners.

For starters, mindfulness meditation can help us simply notice our tendency to solidify our thoughts and emotions, to fixate on certain perceptions, and to obsess on particular outcomes in a variety of situations.

In intimate relationships, it's easy to see that flexibility and adaptability are critical. Failed relationships feed on a lack of flexibility and openness by one or both partners. For example, you might have a fixed idea about yourself that you don't like conflict and confrontation. Your partner is asking you to simply show up for a difficult but important communication. Letting go of that idea about yourself could be exactly the right gesture to engage further and work through to a deeper connection with your partner and your life.

Regarding work and entrepreneurial situations in general, we've so far emphasized clarifying our vision, creating a strategy, creating a solid plan, and executing it. These steps are vitally important to creating a successful business. But here we're adding another element. Even with a clear vision, well-conceived strategy, well-crafted plan, and skillful execution, our project can go off the tracks and into the weeds. As discussed in detail in the previous chapter, the situation can and *will* evolve—circumstances will change, laws will change, employees will change, the weather will change, and *we* will change. Maybe our enthusiasm for the job has waned. Maybe we never really were all that enthusiastic—we just thought of ourselves as the kind of person who *should* love this job. We all operate within the dynamic atmosphere of impermanence and change, and we need to adapt, recalibrate, and shift our perspective and operating system in real time.

In Dharma lingo, we talk about "letting go" as an important part of our mindfulness practice—as in letting go of "sticky" thoughts and emotions as they arise in our practice. We notice them, don't judge or try to analyze or manipulate them; we *let them go* and bring our attention back to our breath and our present awareness. This kind of noticing how we get stuck and learning to let go is more than a way of training our mind; it's also vitally important toward being effective in business and life in general.

When we really start to understand letting go as a way of being, we can begin to notice another quality of reality. Reality is actually shifting so quickly that once we tune in to it, we can almost perceive something unreal and dreamlike about it, even in our everyday experience. In Tantric Buddhism we call this quality the "illusory nature" of reality.

There are practices, related to lucid dreaming, that include tuning in to the direct experience of this dreamlike quality. They're considered advanced, but if you want to explore them on your own time you can read about them. Two good books are *The Tibetan Yogas of Dream and Sleep* by Tenzin Wangyal Rinpoche and *Dream Yoga* by Andrew Holocek: davidnichtern.com/dream

I would just like to add the proviso that if you want to undertake these kinds of practices, find qualified teachers rather than just trying to learn them from a book.

A simpler version of seeing the dreamlike yet vivid experience of our moment-to-moment reality is to consider the possibility that we may not have to take our thick, heavy, solid, well-fortified, embellished, immortalized, ego-centrifugal, maniacally self-involved sense of self so damned seriously. We can all afford to lighten up a bit.

Let's go to your workbook.

22. Not Taking Your Self Too Seriously

1. Can you remember a recent dream you had? If so, recount it in detail.
2. Now do the same thing with an actual "waking" experience you've had within the last several days.
3. Describe the difference between these two experiences. How did you know you were dreaming in the one case and awake in the other?
4. Think about and record the ways in which you might be taking yourself too seriously, ways in which you're rigid, heavy, inflexible, and locked in.
5. Now, to be fair, describe the ways in which you're not taking your situation seriously enough. In what ways might a layer of superficiality and frivolity be covering over something deep and significant, something perhaps you're afraid to face?
6. If you were your best friend, your companion, or your family member, how would you describe ways in which you need to lighten up? You can even ask them and include their comments herein if you want to be really brave!

21 Monitor Your Energy

As soon as you awaken to the power you have, you begin to flex the muscles of your courage. Then you can dream bravely: letting go of your limiting beliefs and pushing past your fears.
> —ALBERTO VILLOLDO, *Courageous Dreaming: How Shamans Dream the World into Being*

I N ANY SITUATION, taking note of our energy level can be incredibly revealing. Some activities and interactions increase our energy, and some deplete us. Have you ever had a conversation with somebody and right after noticed that you feel tired and drained? Or even during? Often these fluctuations are happening just below the conscious level of our awareness, but if we learn to monitor our energy we can begin to really notice it rising and falling.

One of the interesting things about meditating is that it leaves us ample space and time to simply observe the movement and energy of our state of mind without judgment or manipulation. It gives us a way to simply see what's on our mind, literally, rather than blindly following every random thought into the world of emotional reactivity and then action.

One benefit of becoming more aware of our state of mind is that we can learn to monitor, access, cultivate, and elevate our energetic states as well. One of the surefire signs of a great meditation master is that they have a tremendous—at times, almost magical—energy level. Some of the great teachers I've studied with almost kind of glow. It's like they're in the center of a large and luminous energy field.

Other people might also exude this kind of expansive energy: charismatic entertainers, musicians, athletes, politicians, etc. An important distinction to watch out for is that the energy of a truly great master should always feel benevolent. In some people, there can be tremendous energy and charisma, but there can also be lots of ego mixed in with it, as well as manipulation and self-aggrandizement. Of course, we can also find this mix of great energy and charisma together with pride and ego-tripping in spiritual teachers, where the combo can be especially toxic and even potentially dangerous—just a little warning there for all of us who put out a shingle in the meditation biz.

In regard to monitoring our energy, sometimes in meditation we use the analogy of the mind being like a horse. A horse is a powerful animal, but a human being can, potentially, tame it and even ride it. Meditation is sometimes described as being like the saddle we place on the horse of mind, so we can communicate with it skillfully, without being aggressive, clingy, or spaced out.

You could say that the evolution of meditation practice starts with the horse (our mind) riding us (doesn't that seem like what stress, anxiety, and confusion feel like?), becomes us riding the horse with discipline and awareness, and then evolves further toward us being in command of our horse—powerfully and skillfully mastering and enjoying the full range and capacity of our human experience.

In the Tibetan tradition, there's even the notion of riding the energy of the horse of our mind so skillfully that it begins to feel that such a powerful horse can actually fly—literally called "windhorse," or *lungta*, in Tibetan—rather like Pegasus in the Greek tradition, al-Buraq in Islam, and Chollima in Korean lore.

Certain practices within the Shambhala tradition are intended to "raise" our windhorse and uplift our energy in order to fearlessly meet the challenge of living. These practices range in content and complexity, but the simple idea is to rouse ourselves with good posture, focus our mind in the current situation, and radiate out a feeling of confidence, power, and strength.

Even though this practice seems quite simple, it's best to learn such things from qualified teachers, to avoid pitfalls. For example, we all know that it's possible to feel increased energy from arrogance, aggression, lust, and competition, but that's not what we're talking about here. The kind of confidence generated by windhorse practices is based on the solid foundation of training in mindfulness and compassion.

Let's go to your workbook.

23. Monitoring Your Energy

1. Tap into your energy *right now*. Describe how you feel. Energetic? Enthusiastic? Speedy? Anxious? Depressed? Exhausted? Drained? Fried? Happy? Peaceful? Calm?
2. See if you can locate that feeling in your physical body. If so, please describe.
3. Identify and describe the thoughts that accompany that feeling.
4. Take a really strong upright seat. See if you can trigger a feeling of strong presence. Right now. Right here in this very moment. Can you cut through that feeling you identified in step 1 above? If so, where did it go? Write down any observations you can about any aspect of these experiences.

Sometimes our windhorse practice will fall flat because our body is simply too run down and we're too physically exhausted to mount up and ride properly. Physical health can be an important support for our overall psychological and emotional well-being. (For more on this, see chapter 23.) Having said that, I've been amazed at times to find myself on the road, traveling sometimes for twenty-four hours straight or more, ending up in an upside-down time zone, and still able to hit the ground running. (Or sitting, as I sometimes like to say!)

I attribute this kind of resilience to mindfulness, qigong, and windhorse practices. We often have lots of energy in reserve, and we can tap it. A huge part of the generation of this kind of energy is simply not struggling against what is—we can be fluid and adaptable if we don't resist or complain about our situation. In Buddhism, effort mixed with a joyful attitude can open up energy fields beyond what we previously assumed to be our limitation.

22 Make Friends with Yourself

If You Don't, Nobody Else Can or Will

If you've ever wished for a friend who would love you as you are, appreciate your genius, and make space for your foibles . . . well, I can introduce you to this person . . . You are the one you've been waiting for, as they say.

—SUSAN PIVER, *Start Here Now: An Open-Hearted Guide to the Path and Practice*

I'VE BEEN TEACHING meditation for over forty years. In my public workshops, I'm like an elementary school teacher in a way: I work with beginners and even brand-new beginners at least 80 percent of the time.

My job, as I see it, is

1. to somehow create enough interest, through language, imagery, social media, personal contact, etc., so people will actually show up at these workshops;
2. to give clear and accessible instructions so that beginners can catch a glimpse of what meditation is, what it's good for, and how to do it;
3. to encourage people to create a regular practice (irregular practice creates irregular results); and
4. in some cases, to continue to mentor those individuals and assist them in staying "on the path" and evolving their practice and its flowering in their everyday lives.

We Buddhist teachers mostly agree that the three biggest obstacles (aside from actually acquiring a meditation cushion) to someone starting to develop a meditation practice are these:

1. Getting to that cushion (on a regular basis)
2. Receiving and then remembering clear instructions
3. Having enough gentleness and kindness toward themselves to lean in and stay with it, even when the going gets tough—which often is right away

This last one's a biggie. Practicing mindfulness and sticking with this practice is challenging! It actually *is* a game-changer, but most of us will experience frustration, boredom, irritation, doubt, anxiety, and any and every other feeling we've ever had, were never comfortable with, and have been running away from for most of our lives.

The ads that tout mindfulness centers and mindfulness trainings as the panacea for our problems are simply not mentioning this small fact, just as the ads for gyms and fitness centers don't mention that getting in shape involves meeting and accepting our minds and bodies in the exact shape they're currently in, making friends with them, having some kind of sympathy and appreciation for ourselves, and *developing the discipline* of leaning into a practice. We have some idea that this effort will be good for us but perhaps we would rather do something else, such as eat ice cream, watch TV, social mediate (instead of meditate), and generally just keep doing what we're used to doing. This is exactly what the ads are not telling us.

Here's our slogan again from chapter 2:

> With meditation practice there are various benefits, but none of them can be realized if you don't **make the time to actually practice.**

Any practice is challenging. Try learning to play the violin in three easy lessons. Try becoming a great tennis player overnight. Try learning Japanese or Russian. There's no magic. It takes effort.

So many of my students negotiate with themselves and then with me to shorten their sessions. Some have a really hard time sitting for even five minutes a day. Very, very few students have said, "I'm thinking of lengthening my meditation sessions, perhaps going from twenty minutes a day to a full hour on the weekend. Would that be OK?" If we're gentle, we can be really curious about why it can be so hard just to be with ourselves in this simple and raw way. We can stay with the practice rather than running away from it.

In the effort to practice mindfulness, we'll develop clarity, strength of mind, and stability (just like the ads say), but we'll also have to face our own mind and heart without a whole lot of padding. The practice is so simple and there we are—naked and wriggling.

Meditation is a way to genuinely make friends with ourselves, warts and all, and develop ourselves as human beings. Too much ambition, too much aggression, too much agenda, and we'll find ourselves getting tighter and tighter.

Instead we can try to relax and treat ourselves kindly, which will be challenging for many of us. But as Trungpa Rinpoche often repeated—I can still hear his high-pitched Tibetan/Oxonian accent—"YOU CAN DO IT!" And you can.

Please go to your workbook:

24. Making Friends with Yourself

1. Have you noticed during your mindfulness practice any of the following obstacles?
   a. Irritation
   b. Boredom
   c. Doubt

    d. Fatigue

    e. Resistance

2. Have you also noticed any of the following positive qualities?

    a. Tenderness

    b. Curiosity

    c. Appreciation of your life

    d. Gratitude

    e. Gentleness

    f. Fearlessness

    g. A lessening of judgment and harsh self-criticism

If the answer is yes, to anything on these lists—good! You're doing it right.

23 Self-Deception Is the Final Frontier

Develop Clarity about Your Own Negative Habits and Weaknesses

The unexamined life is not worth living.
—SOCRATES

A s WE DEVELOP our meditation practice, at times it will seem like a long and winding road. We're not sure if we're one step forward, two steps back, or off the path completely and lost in the woods.

But I think we'll find that the whole journey is completely workable if we're simply honest with ourselves. Seeing ourselves clearly is so difficult. It seems as if it should be the easiest thing to do; after all, we've logged in tremendous hours with ourselves: we eat with ourselves, we go the bathroom with ourselves, we even sleep with ourselves. We are, by any measure, totally intimate with ourselves—far more than with any other sentient being we know.

And yet, to a very considerable extent, despite all that contact, we remain somewhat of a mystery to ourselves. We're even surprised sometimes by our own thoughts, feelings, and dreams; we feel as if they were emanating from someplace other than our own mind. The whole predicament is, as *Star Trek*'s Mr. Spock would say, "Fascinating."

There's no doubt that, beyond creating stability and focus, meditation is a path, a method, that allows us to penetrate further into the mystery of our own existence. It can help us understand how our mind works and how our sense of reality is constructed. The approach isn't theoretical or remote; it's very scientific. We just eliminate distractions and spend time directly observing our own mind.

We've already discussed the obstacle of not being kind and gentle enough, but there's another one: our limitless capability to play hide-and-seek with ourselves. We're capable of engaging in layers and layers of denial and self-deception. It's impossible not to uncover this tendency if we go deep enough with our practice.

Essentially, meditation is a very special kind of mirror we hold up so we can see ourselves clearly, move beyond harsh self-criticism and denial, and begin to peel back the layers of false notions we hold about who and what we are. It's said that subtler and subtler layers of self-deception and denial are with us until the very end of our journey, and experienced meditators should become more and more sensitive to this possibility—especially teachers!

John Welwood, a psychotherapist who was also a student of Trungpa Rinpoche, coined the phrase *spiritual bypassing*: the "tendency to use spiritual ideas and practices to sidestep or avoid facing unresolved emotional issues, psychological wounds, and unfinished developmental tasks."

Here's a link to the interview with John, called "Human Nature, Buddha Nature," where he offers that definition, if you're curious: davidnichtern.com/bypass

In my teacher-training programs, a central theme we try to impart to aspiring teachers is to self-assess regularly, gauging our aspiration, inspiration, motivation, perspiration, and realization. Finally, we're asked to consider the possibility that we don't know what we don't know—like a blind spot for which we need an extra mirror (which can be our own teachers or friends or our practice). If we look into such a mirror and find ourselves making adjustments and excuses, we should consider pausing and allowing the actual clear image to come through, blemishes and all. That's good practice but very challenging to do.

One way to check our level of realization is to simply watch our own mind with our own family at Thanksgiving dinner—where our karma is right there in our face, right next to the turkey (tofurkey for the vegetarians perhaps) and sweet potatoes.

When we engage in a process of self-discovery, it's often the case that our *aha!* moments are recognitions of that which was already present; we see the deeper feelings that underlie what we consider to be our emotional landscape. When we let go of those layers, we might experience a kind of rawness and vulnerability that we're simply not used to. That's why in our practice, sometimes, we can feel that we're becoming more exposed and more vulnerable.

This kind of experience is progress on our spiritual journey, even though it may not feel that way at first. It's also the case that this raw and exposed substrata can become the foundation and source of genuine confidence and courage.

Let's go to your workbook.

25. Denial and Self-Deception

1. Consider self-deception. How do you deceive others? How do you deceive yourself?

   This will be an interesting exercise since nobody else really cares what you write here. In fact, nobody else is even aware of what you're going to say. You can even cross this out after you write it down so even your heirs won't be able to read it after you're dead and they find this workbook in your attic underneath that high school yearbook that you have had there for fifty years!

2. What do you think it is that keeps you from being honest

about your blemishes with yourself? I'm not talking about immortalizing them with some kind of litany of self-pity here; instead, simply acknowledge them without beating the horse the insight rode in on.

3. What's the main reason that it's so hard to be honest about your flaws with others? Pride? Embarrassment? Dread? ✎

We're not trying to put shrinks out of work here, but a little bit of freestyle self-exploration might save us a few extra visits, no?

24 Train Your Mind, Train Your Body

Mindfulness Is the Foundation of Enlightened Living

Peace in the world starts with peace in oneself. If everyone lives mindfully, everyone will be more healthy, feel more fulfilled in their daily lives, and there will be more peace.

—THICH NHAT HANH

IN ADDITION TO all the practices of mind and spirit we've discussed in this book, it's also important that we respect and care for our body.

My mother used to say, "Be true to your teeth or they'll be false to you." Of course, she had a particular style of humor, but that kind of approach is good for us at all levels. Here's a similar story: I've been studying with a wonderful tai chi teacher, Master Sat Hon, for almost twenty years now. When I mentioned to Master Hon that after turning seventy I was waiting to see which of my organs would betray me, he turned it around and said that it would be me betraying them—which is not that divergent from my mother's comment!

We aren't talking about self-cherishing and narcissism here but rather a healthy and balanced approach to living in our body. Obviously this attitude will depend on the body we currently have and will perhaps involve letting go of an overly idealized version that only brings us pain and disappointment.

Many of us are, to borrow a phrase from yoga practice, externally rotated. By that I mean that we tend to view our lives as reflected by our external circumstances—we can get caught up in how we think we appear. There's nothing wrong with external verification—earlier we said that everybody wants to be and should be appreciated—but there's something much more fundamental to our well-being than any form of external confirmation: how we actually feel. Our relationship to our body and mind is what finally determines whether we're truly happy; otherwise we'll be eternally waiting for an Academy Award or the like to verify our sense of worth and accomplishment.

As warriors, in the Shambhala sense of the term, we can recognize that our body and mind are our primary assets and we need to take good care of them. I've often used the metaphor, when teaching meditation, of taking our mind to the gym. We spend our whole life stuffing our mind (and body, for that matter) with content, but we rarely work with training our mind (or body, for that matter). A possible analogy is getting a proper tune-up—in this case, once a day for fifteen to twenty minutes. Just work with our basic state of mind and clean it up, flush it out, and refresh the lube.

So when you wake up next Thursday morning, just check in and see how your body feels, how your *whole* body feels, and then check in on your state of mind. Keep it simple and direct.

Meditation is good for your mind *and* body, and mindful exercise (any kind) is good for your body *and* mind. When mind and body are synchronized, you'll lead a happier and healthier life.

How Do You Feel?

Right now, if you're able, simply take a strong seated position, either on a cushion on the floor or in a chair, and check in with your body and mind. *How do you feel right now?*

You don't have to journal or try to keep track for later, just get in touch in this moment and check yourself out.

You can start by scanning your body if you like, part by part, or simply just gauge the overall physical feeling. Notice any tightness, pain, itching, tension, even pleasurable sensations. It's not necessary, but if you prefer, you can just release some of the tension you find as you find it. That will turn this exercise from a simple awareness practice into a relaxation technique, but why not? It's not a crime to relax, and sometimes it can be the best medicine.

The important point, however, is just to bring your body into the field of present awareness and see what's going on, without judgment or too much elaboration and manipulation.

Then you can tune in to your mind, which includes your thoughts, your emotions, any superficial narrative, and the images and movies that are flashing through on their way from wherever to wherever. It could be as simple as noticing that you're feeling anxious or sad. Once again, try not to analyze or manipulate too much. You're just taking your temperature, in a manner of speaking.

At some point in your body training, it can be very powerful to simultaneously work with your mental states; and at some point in your meditation training, it can be very important to take on some kind of body practice: yoga, martial arts, any form of sports, etc.

When you're working with your mind through mindfulness or other meditation techniques, it can be so helpful to bring that training all the way down to the level of your actual earthly body, if at all possible.

Sometime after the Buddha attained enlightenment, he famously encountered his old yoga buddies in the forest. It seemed to them that the Buddha had an unusual radiance. He was radiating health and strong presence. When they asked him what kind of Dharma, or method, he was now practicing, he declared that he had become enlightened since their last hot yoga sessions. "Wow!" they politely responded. "But how can you verify that? Can you show us the evidence?" Supposedly, as mentioned previously, he reached down and touched the earth, which shook in recognition of his accomplishment. This is a charming story, and we can take it literally if we choose to. But as a metaphor, it has ongoing profound and inescapable meaning: wisdom is at the body level—the level of earth.

We've been talking about developing knowledge and insight, but it's particularly important to bring that wisdom all the way down to the ground and manifest it in the realm of form and action. The quality of our presence and sense of physical well-being can often totally trump any attempt we make to convince people through narrative or philosophy.

When someone has developed real wisdom, you can feel it as a tangible physical presence. They have become deeply grounded and the result is what we would call "wisdom embodied," *jnanasattva* in Sanskrit. Great masters such as my teacher, CTR, have a really powerful vibration, but they're also deeply rooted in their bodies and communicating wisdom in every moment by how they handle the physical world. CTR was so connected to his body that when he poured a cup of tea, it was every bit as profound as one of his deepest Dharma talks.

Master Hon has a great expression: "Bodies don't lie." Our bodies tell the truth. As meditators, teachers, leaders, creatives, lovers, parents, citizens, and yogis, we should learn to read body language—our own and others'.

When I talk to my friends in the fitness and sports universe, they usually confirm that the future of fitness is mind-body integration. So when we're assessing our own practice, our own development, it can be really helpful to create a practice of mind and body training, where each is in balance with the other.

I think we can easily see that if we take care of our body as if it were a separate entity, we may get strong, flexible, and energetic, but our mind may still be weak, stiff, and fried. Master Hon calls certain kinds of physically developed athletes in the West "lobsters." They have a strong outer shell, but the inner *organs* and vital energy (chi) are weak and disconnected.

Our mind-body integration is the essence of our power, strength, vitality, and resourcefulness. We should treat both with equal respect and discipline.

Let's go to your workbook.

26. Mind and Body

1. How is your body feeling overall these days?
2. Do you have some kind of regular physical practice? If not, what kind of practice could you see yourself adopting?
3. Do you have any form of integrated mind-body practice? If so, please describe. If not, what kind of practice could you see yourself adopting?
4. How connected do you feel to your body? Do you feel deeply rooted? Or disconnected, as if you're a head floating in space?
5. Are you obsessed with your body and taking seriously good care of it, but feeling, honestly, somewhat detached from it emotionally and energetically? Do you go to the gym and train your body while your mind is reading the paper, watching the news, and texting your friends, all at the same time?

25 Actually Drain the Swamp

Overcome Poverty Mentality and Find Your Authentic Confidence

The key to warriorship and the first principle of Shambhala vision is not being afraid of who you are. Ultimately, that is the definition of bravery: not being afraid of yourself.

—CHÖGYAM TRUNGPA, *Shambhala: The Sacred Path of the Warrior*

AS ALREADY MENTIONED, Trungpa Rinpoche often used the phrase *poverty mentality* to express a loss of confidence in our basic being. When we experience poverty mentality, we don't feel competent, empowered, loved, or respected. Our mind has become like a swamp in which even uplifting possibilities get pulled into a dark and funky brew of self-doubt, hopelessness, and regret.

If you've never experienced these kinds of feelings, you can skip this chapter. Otherwise read on.

If we recognize a pattern of poverty mentality in ourselves, what can we do about it? Such a mindset seems to create its own energy and momentum, a field effect in which we feel depleted, defeated, and unseated. It undermines our vitality, confidence, and stability.

So here are a few steps to consider if we're suffering from poverty mentality. You can think of each of these as a slogan, if you like.

1. Bring awareness to the situation.

As a meditation student and teacher, I've seen so many elaborate and complicated schemes for psychological and spiritual development. So instead, I would like to offer a bone-simple approach to meditation sessions and, in fact, to premeditation and postmeditation sessions (in other words your actual life): bring awareness to whatever you're experiencing.

If you're feeling good, bring awareness to those thoughts and sensations. If you feel life sucks and you're contemplating suicide, bring awareness to those thoughts and sensations. If you're feeling numb, dull, indifferent, cynical, hypercritical, ecstatic, curious, depressed, elated, inspired, hopeless—whatever you're experiencing—bring awareness to those myriad expressions of having a body and mind.

A body and mind without awareness is called a zombie, and a body and mind suffused with awareness is called a buddha. Awareness is the most powerful game-changer we can access.

By "bringing awareness" we mean cultivating the totally organic quality of noticing, in the present moment, what we're thinking and feeling—without judgment, evaluation, or manipulation. *This is what is currently called mindfulness.* Mindfulness is trending heavily in our contemporary international community for a reason—it's a game-changer.

When we Buddhists refer to "sentient beings" (which includes but isn't limited to human beings), we're referring to this capacity for self-awareness. It's the key to our continued growth and evolution, both as individuals and as the human species.

> 2. To bring awareness to your situation, cultivate the art
> of attention. Learn how to place, direct, and focus your
> attention.

Since the possibility of awareness—of ourselves and of the entire situation in which we find ourselves—is always present, why do we spend so much time in dull and distracted states of mind, lacking awareness?

We can think of self-awareness as a kind of light and clarity that's constantly present but disregarded or covered over by strong habitual tendencies and patterns. Perhaps a good analogy is that awareness is like the light in whatever room you're in right now. It's wired, flowing, and always potentially shining, but you have to actually flip the switch to activate it.

Attention, and in particular learning how to place our attention, is the key to flipping that switch to turn on our awareness. The spearhead of most meditation training, and for that matter physical training, is to place our attention and flip the switch so that awareness can awaken and flow through.

3. Hone your intention.

Attention may be the key to flipping the switch of awareness from off to on, but *intention* is the key to remembering to find and flip that switch. Without clarifying and strengthening our intention, it's likely that we'll simply skip over the glorious opportunity to wake up and fully tune in to our awareness mind.

By force of inertia, we tend to linger in dull, unconscious states of mind, chasing our own projections in a cascade of expectation and disappointment. Buddhists call this inertia *samsara*: the habitual patterns that trap us (as discussed in chapter 3).

The schematics of samsara was the focus of my last book, called *Awakening from the Daydream*, if you'd like to check it out: davidnichtern.com/daydream

4. Respect your mind and your body.

Respect is such a great concept. Remember the late, great Aretha Franklin singing, "Find out what you mean to me"? We show our respect by treating the object of our respect with care, awareness, and precision. We don't take the object of our respect for granted.

5. Respect other people's minds and bodies.

Respecting others' bodies and minds should flow gracefully and naturally from self-respect.

6. Move toward the light and keep going.

In the Buddhist tradition, awareness is sometimes identified with luminosity. When we bring the light of awareness to whatever we experience, it can feel as if the world is glowing, suffused with light and energy. This isn't some kind of New Age fantasy. For instance, the notion of moving toward the light is the basis of all plant life on earth.

7. Rouse a sense of confidence and uplifted energy.

We've discussed this already, so this is just a reminder to monitor your energy and raise your windhorse when you need it.

These are a few suggestions as to how to become aware of our own poverty mentality, acknowledge it, and then lean into a more uplifted, positive, and confident state of mind.

Let's go to your workbook.

27. Recognizing and Overcoming Poverty Mentality

1. Can you identify with the notion of poverty mentality? Have you ever experienced it firsthand? What did it feel like? What was the quality of that experience?
2. When you're trapped in that state of mind, how does it feel? Does it feel temporary, that it will shift? Or does it feel like the last stop on the fast track to nowhere?
3. Describe any particular narrative threads that usually accompany a feeling of poverty mentality. Are there particular story lines that keep coming back to certify a sense of worthlessness and defeat?
4. Can you also identify a particular comfort zone that these states provide for you? If so, please describe. In the Shambhala teachings we call this the cocoon—it's warm and funky and messy but it feels like home.
5. How do you imagine it feels to step out of the cocoon, out of your poverty mentality? Is there a feeling of being a little bit more exposed, a little more vulnerable, like stepping into a less familiar landscape? Good!

Part **VI** Creativity:
The Wild Card

FINALLY! I KNOW what you're thinking: "Dave—creativity is the first topic in your title and you're just now getting to it? I'm exhausted reading about all this other stuff. What took you so long?!"
Well . . . I have two things to say:

1. We've been talking about creativity all along. Creativity is really the thread underlying this whole conversation. It's creative to discover and make your offering. It's creative to bring your offering to the marketplace. It's creative to explore your own mind and body. It's creative to wake up in the morning. It's creative to dream in the night. Life is creativity itself!
2. If you don't like any of those answers, how about this one: save the best for last!

OK, here we go. We're going to take a leap, but I think you'll see that many of the same principles we've already discussed will continue to apply. Let's see . . .

26 Forget Everything You Read in This Book

Every single thing I have done as a creative person
has been an accident.

—JAMIE LEE CURTIS

FINALLY, AS PROMISED, we're going to zoom in on the creativity piece of our discussion. So far we've been so good, so rational, so reasonable, so wise, so intelligent. Now we're going to have a chance to be bad, unreasonable, impulsive, irrational, a little bit wild, and maybe even a little bit weird.

I always have a laugh when somebody in one of my workshops says, "I'm not creative." Living and getting through a day means you're already fundamentally creative. Choosing a pair of socks or a hairdo or an eyeglasses frame is creative. Making dinner or ordering take-out is creative. Creativity is what happens when we make choices; we have to feel and then act, choose a direction. Our whole life is a creative process whether we see it that way or not.

We've already explored the three-stage process of creating an offering, making a plan, and taking it to the marketplace. But here we're just taking a peek at the moment of inception, when a creative idea dawns and sparks, seemingly coming from nowhere at all.

Ironically, this stage of the creative process mirrors our meditation practice, in which we don't hold on to thoughts and emotions but release them into a strong vibrant feeling of present awareness. This open space is also the space from whence creativity, intuition, even divination can arise. It's a lot like what the Zen peeps call "not-knowing." We rest our mind in an open and spacious way, and from that inception can arise. As Master Hon says, "Embrace uncertainty."

Trungpa Rinpoche used to say, "First thought, best thought." He has a book of poetry by that name, and we used to create poetry on the spot with him—sometimes as a group with each person contributing a line. The process was intensely spontaneous and light as opposed to deliberative and heavy. It also felt edgy and provocative.

Once we create something, further development includes perfecting our business skills: planning, discipline, effort, execution, and completion. Every activity, including our life itself, seems to share the same rhythm—emptiness, inception, birth, development, fruition, release, and back to emptiness. Any musical sound, for that matter, contains space, inception, evolution, sustain, decay, and release.

We'll explore this evolutionary process as we go deeper into the relationship between creativity and manifesting. But for now, let's just see if we can find something fun to say about inception—capturing "lightning in a bottle."

For me, I get creative ideas at odd times, often in the shower, sometimes while meditating, in the twilight between sleep and awake, sometimes in dreams, often also inspired by feelings of love, surrender, and affection. It's unpredictable.

I saw Neil Young give a talk years ago, in which he attempted to describe the process of creativity. I believe he used the commonly applied metaphor of courting the muse. The muse is receptive, magically appearing and disappearing, catalytic, and impetuous. Neil said that when the muse called, he had to go—even if he was supposed to pick up his kid at school. If a song came zooming into his mind, he had to turn the car around, head to the studio, and put on his catcher's mitt to receive the muse's pitch.

I'm sure he made other arrangements those times for childcare, but I resonated with his comments. In any case, the story serves as an excellent metaphor for creative types—we're on call, and it can be really productive to respond in some way when the muse sends a text. For that reason, sometimes creative types can be a little irresponsible, even narcissistic. Of course, since we're talking about an integrated lifestyle here, balance is recommended.

I'm going to give an example from my own life to show the atmosphere of inception, when an idea is coming out of nowhere and we put out our butterfly net and make the attempt to catch it.

In my life I've functioned in many creative and professional capacities, but one significant thread has been as a composer and songwriter. I still think of this area (music in general, composing in particular) as my most natural gift, and if I don't access it from time to time I start to feel constipated and unhappy.

In the 1970s I was an aspiring songwriter and was working as a guitar player and sometimes music director for a variety of singers making the rounds. It was a colorful time; so many of us were exploring new creative and spiritual forms simultaneously. At one point I had a band with Jerry Garcia and David Grisman, and sometimes right after a gig I would fly somewhere to spend time with CTR. When I think about that now, I just can't believe how fortunate I was to be able to go back and forth between two such incredibly rich creative environments.

So there I am, being a singer-songwriter in New York City, playing various gigs by myself and with others, writing some songs, and teaching guitar to augment my marginal income. I had a girlfriend at the time who lived uptown. She actually had a waterbed! I think waterbeds went the way of cassettes . . . you don't really see them around much anymore.

One night, after a wonderful and adventurous gambit on this floating oasis of blissful encounters, we had some hummus, grape leaves, feta, and pita for a little snack. I reached over and grabbed her Martin 000-28 guitar and in real time created the basic content and structure for "Midnight at the Oasis." The song was almost complete immediately, though I did further craft the lyrics on my next road trip.

Why am I telling you this story?

1. Because it was fun to do and is fun to tell.
2. It's illustrating my point about how spontaneous creativity is and how we shouldn't really work too hard at it. It's better to relax, enter the flow, and get out your catcher's mitt.

I think I made around two to three million dollars over several decades from this playful little song. Tell that to your parents the next time they insist you go back to law or medical school so you can earn a living.

Ironically, the revenue generated from that one simple ditty allowed me to take serious time off from the music biz to study Buddhism intensively.

I visited Los Angeles later in my life (maybe the late '90s) and went to see my old mentor and record company legend Lenny Waronker, who had believed in my song and produced the record. He gave me my shot, and when I thought about him in later years and started my own record labels, I wanted to be like Lenny and give young artists their shot.

I wanted to express my gratitude to him. On the way to his office I stopped and bought a beautiful antique Japanese sake set and wrapped it along with the following spontaneous haiku (well, not a real haiku, more like a poem, but haiku sounds better):

Past, present and future
In a drop of sake
Thank you for financing
My Buddhist education!

I left his office before he opened the gift, because I didn't want to put him on the spot. I hope he liked it!

Now let's go to your workbook.

 ## 28. Creativity and You

1. What does creativity mean to you? What's your connection to it? Can you relate to the wild-card aspect we're discussing here?
2. Do you feel that you have creativity lurking in you and don't have the right circumstances to express yourself? If so, what do you need to get at it—a hug, a squeeze, a push, more time, more space?
3. Is your creative output a hobby or part of your livelihood?
4. If it's your hobby, do you contemplate developing it further and making it part of your livelihood equation?
5. If so, how do you plan to combine creativity and livelihood?
6. How would you express your creativity as part of or as connected to your spiritual journey in this life? Feel free to answer this question any way you like.

27 Be Daring

The Dignity of Outrageous

Fortunately, my parents always said, "You know what, you don't have to decide what you're going to be, ever. You can be something different every day if you want."

—LAURIE ANDERSON

IN THE SHAMBHALA teachings, there are many groupings of symbolic representations. One of these sets represents the evolution of an aspiring warrior; it's called the *four dignities*: meek, perky, outrageous, and inscrutable.

Each of the four dignities is represented by an animal (real or mythical) that embodies the virtue we're seeking to cultivate. *Meek* is represented by a tiger, symbolizing the power of humbleness and mindfulness, which overcome arrogance and self-importance. *Perky* is represented by a snow lion, which is said to be able to leap from mountaintop to mountaintop and represents the quality of freshness and delight—this is very much related to "first thought, best thought" mentioned in the previous chapter. *Outrageous* is embodied by the garuda, the mythical Indian hawk that hatches from its egg fully grown and never needs to land. The garuda flies beyond conventional reference points and doesn't need approval for its actions. Its shriek can break through predictable thoughts and attitudes. Finally, the dragon represents the dignity of *inscrutable*. It's not that the dragon is hiding something or playing a game but rather that its mind is so vast that it's difficult to fathom. It can be totally strategic but unpredictable at the same time.

The four dignities are a beautiful scheme for cultivating power-ful qualities in our lives. As part of our discussion about creativity, we're going to look more closely at the garuda: the symbol of being outrageous and daring.

When inception first arises, it may not make sense in a linear kind of way, or it might make *perfect* sense, even *transcendental* sense. Picasso comes to mind immediately. I once sat and looked at his painting *Guernica* for about an hour. I was overwhelmed by how out-rageous it was but also how completely grounded it felt and how clearly it told the story. His art was shocking to the senses but so easy to decipher on another level. Outrageous can, at times, make perfect sense.

The reason we're bringing the quality of outrageous here is that, at the end of the day, we have to *dare* to be creative. Even the word itself—*creativity*—indicates that we're not satisfied with what already exists and are going to *create* something else.

Sometimes when we dare to be creative, we might recognize that we have, unintentionally, recreated something that already exists. That is, assuming we're not crassly and intentionally ripping off someone else's creativity—that's called *stealing*.

As we were saying, creativity is fundamentally daring and outra-geous. As I write, my partner, Monika, is decorating our little beach cabin in Thailand with Hindu deities and a variety of flowers. Flower arranging is a particularly outrageous activity; we create these beauti-ful settings knowing full well that they will only last several days. The Hindu deities might last a bit longer. ☺

At one retreat I attended in Maui, there was a panel discussion led by Duncan Trussell with Sharon Salzberg, Jack Kornfield, and Raghu Markus. Duncan had just interviewed me for his podcast, and I had described the Buddhist notion of impermanence in some detail. So he went to the panel and said, "Well, Nichtern said that even the Hindu deities are impermanent." Hanuman is impermanent? Boy, did that light up a discussion! If even our gods are impermanent, what, if any, reference points can we hold on to? It's a profound contemplation. Usually our God, gods, are untouchable. Without them we have even less of an idea of who we are than we did before. Anyhow—remember—your guess is as good as mine. ☺

In any case, impermanence is an important element of creativity. We know that nothing *we* create will actually last. It's part of the energy of creativity. Some forms of expression rely heavily on that understanding—like jazz, for example, or sports, cooking, or dance. None of these things last and yet we're drawn to expressing ourselves in such a wide variety of ways.

Often, in order to create something, we have to take a kind of leap. "Crazy wisdom" is a style of teaching embedded in the Tibetan Buddhist tradition. Trungpa Rinpoche was said to be a holder of that kind of lineage. It's important to understand that this is an actual lineage and a very highly trained type of master. Just improvising and acting strange doesn't qualify you as a crazy wisdom teacher, especially if you're causing further confusion and harm through your actions.

If you study jazz, you can begin to understand crazy wisdom. Innovation is based on thoroughly understanding the classical tradition your innovation emerges from. There's a huge difference between Ornette Coleman blowing "free" and some untrained kid with a sax and a bucket playing on the street corner blowing "free." This might sound arrogant, but in our tradition there's no freedom without discipline and training; freedom is a final stage.

CTR used to say that the exact translation of *crazy wisdom* into English would more accurately be described as *wisdom crazy*. The wisdom is so profound that it can move beyond conventional boundaries. The reason I'm including this discussion here is that creativity, in some sense, always has an element of crazy wisdom.

As Apple's famous campaign so brilliantly stated, "Think different."

Of course, the grammatically correct way to say that would be "think differently"—that's part of the creativity and the compelling quality of the message.

Creativity is, by definition, always breaking the established norms and boundaries. All governmental forms emerged from the creativity of the human mind addressing social configurations. All technological innovation comes from dismantling previous paradigms. Every sport we play was dreamed up by some goofy enthusiast; every hobby, every dish we eat, every word we say, every instrument we play is the product of somebody's enthusiasm, daring, and crazy wisdom. Creativity is unfathomable. To understand it is to understand life itself.

Let's go to your workbook.

29. Creativity and Daring

1. How do you feel and react when it comes to daring to leap into new territory? Hesitant? Doubtful? Anxious? Overly excited? Disciplined? Write about your relationship to making that leap into creative space.
2. Who are a few of your favorite role models for being creative, daring, and outrageous?
3. How do you feel when you want to take that leap but hesitate and back away?
4. Do you think you're a creative person? Why or why not?
5. Do you think you should be more constrained and disciplined, or do you feel that you need to be more daring and take more chances?

28 Know Where You Are on the Timeline

All Drama Has a Beginning, Middle, and End

Our proposal is that tragedy is the imitation of a complete and whole deed, and one that has some kind of magnitude (since it's possible for a thing to be whole and to lack magnitude). A story that's whole has a beginning, middle, and an end.

—ARISTOTLE, *Poetics*

LIKE POSSIBLY many of you, I have creative ideas at all hours of the day and night, including in dreams! Potential projects seem to just pop into my mind and take shape; it's almost as if I'm an attendant, observer, even innocent bystander. An entire song for the musical I'm writing came to me in a dream; all I did was write it down when I woke up. It was already intact—beginning, middle, and end.

I think we've established that creativity is a wild card. However, in this chapter I'd like to share a few thoughts about follow-through—about bringing a creative project all the way from inception to manifestation. The full process is similar, in some ways, to raising a child or creating any kind of new enterprise.

As above, Aristotle said that all drama has a beginning, middle, and end; all drama (maybe life too) is essentially a three-act play. As my friend screenwriter Stanley Weiser (*Wall Street* and *W.*, among others) says, "Act 1 we introduce our characters, act 2 get them up a tree, and act 3 get them down."

Having a creative idea is a flash or burst, leaning into the project to bring it along is hard work, and actually finishing is a serious accomplishment. The stage of bringing it to the marketplace, if that's our choice, is yet another journey and is mostly covered in the making-a-buck section you just read. Even though the initial stages of creation might seem closer to voodoo or science fiction, once we're underway, all the more practical principles we've already discussed will come to bear.

So let's take a look at the three stages of drama as it relates to the three stages of cooking up a creative idea and bringing it to fruition—with an optional bonus fourth stage of bringing it to market. This discussion also might remind you of our ground, path, and fruition concept from chapter 9.

1. INCEPTION / CONCEPTION

Here the metaphor of falling in love works pretty well. There's a feeling of stimulation, arousal, that's almost abstract—haunting, beguiling, something is reaching out to us, sending signals, making suggestive noises and gestures.

Then suddenly, almost instantaneously, a visualization, an idea, springs into our mind. We've already mentioned "first thought, best thought"; a fresh thought comes into our mind, not as a result of digging hard, working on it, and pulling it out, but spontaneously, more intuitively, suddenly.

Here's a link to a video of me talking about first thought. It might be helpful to view it to zero in on this concept of inception: davidnichtern.com/thought

That first thought has the quality of inception. It could just be a passing notion or piece of information, or it could feel as if there's a further implication, something to work with, to develop.

For me, sometimes these ideas are surprisingly evolved. It's as if they come from nowhere, but there's a feeling that in some other realm they already exist full-blown. Now, for an instant, there's an opportunity to pull them into this time, this place.

2. DEVELOPMENT

If the inception lingers in some way, if it invites further exploration or evolution, it may become some kind of actual creative project for us and begin to marinate in our mind, growing, crystallizing, and taking shape.

Our project may begin to naturally evolve. We may start with "Let's write a song, create a new kind of communication company, or bring existing elements together into a new and unique entity; let's go to Machu Picchu for your birthday; let's change professions, relationships"—you name it.

But as our idea lands, if it sticks around, at some point we'll need to make a further commitment. If we decide to develop our concept further, we might reach a moment where we have to decide whether to lean into our new project with real effort or perhaps abandon ship.

If we lean in, as I'm leaning into writing this book right now, we'll need to really allocate our resources—our precious time and energy—and muster up the discipline to go deeper into the project, working and re-reworking it. Momentum can be so important. Once we have the inspiration, time, and inclination, it can often be most productive to really make an effort—to keep cooking while the ingredients are still fresh.

Importantly, this development stage is most often *less fun* than inception. It's one thing to say, "Let's start a band and become superstars!" and quite another to be on the road for nine months straight, staying in funky motels, four in a room, night after night after night—and not even making enough money to pay your expenses back home.

Development stage isn't really for dreamers anymore. It's a lot of work—hard work. But it can be very rewarding, because we're moving our concept into the realm of tangible manifestation.

3. COMPLETION

At some point, when it comes to creating something, we actually have to finish it. This is true for business plans, raising money, hiring people, firing people, creating paintings, and writing songs, musicals, and movie scripts. It's kind of true about everything.

We've had inception, we've dreamed something up, we've leaned in when all hope seemed lost, and now we have to put down our guitar or pen and let it go. At some point I'll hand this finally edited manuscript you're now reading to my publisher and say, "I'm done. Take my book . . . please!"

Some of us will have a hard time with this part of the process. Imagine working on a symphony for twenty years and you just can't stop tweaking it. Finally you die. It becomes your unfinished symphony.

I have several creative projects on my docket right now. They had inception, I leaned in, I did intense work for a period of time—periodically I'll go back to them for a tweak. But then the wind went out of the sails and I could feel it. I couldn't yet bring them to completion.

Of course, as creative people, we'll always have a set of Tupperware containers filled with half-cooked ventures in the fridge of our mind. There's still the possibility, at any time, of putting one of them back on an active burner and cooking it some more, but we might find that we only infrequently come back to our unfinished symphonies, even those that may have felt full of potential at the time.

Of course, we can also get trapped in the opposite dilemma, which is that our dish may be finished but we continue to cook it, continue to tweak beyond the moment of reasonable completion. This is appropriately called *overcooking the goose.*

We have a saying in sales: "You went past the close." I used to watch my team when I was sales director for New England Digital, and I'd sometimes see them go on and on about how their wonderful relationship with a potential client was evolving, how they were right on the verge of making a deal, and you could just feel that they were going past the close.

Closing is a different move than leaning in. There's a quality of putting that last glaze on the bread, browning it til ready, and then taking it out of the oven and serving it up!

This stage of a creative project can feel a little bit postpartum, even depressing, but it's also a relief and can be exhilarating, because now we enter the fourth stage of the creative process . . . or not! Are we going to take our creation to the market and try to connect this amazing creative process with our livelihood?

Clearly we have two choices at this point. One is to simply enjoy and appreciate the work and share it with whomever we choose to, whenever we choose to. Congratulations! We're some kind of artist, and everybody should be some kind of artist.

However . . .

4. Marketing and Sales

If we're going to become a professional creative, at this point we'll have to take our beloved baby to the market and see if it floats, swims, or drowns.

This part kind of reminds me of taking my son Ethan to Little League in Riverside Park. There he is in his uniform with his cap, bat, and glove, and he's got to go out there and fend for himself. As much as I would have liked to hit the ball and run the bases for him, that would have made me a really uncool and annoying dad for sure.

Now, in the same way, our little project has to fend for itself. If it's a song, we have to actually play it for people—no more talking. If it's a book, we have to hand it in to our publisher (or try to get one) and pray for a good outcome.

If we're creative and *also* good at business, we can do more than pray at this point. We can shift hats again and proactively market and sell our creative output. For many artists, to switch hats in this way can be difficult to impossible.

If that describes you, you're going to need some help—a manager, an agent, a company that specializes in supporting this leg of the journey—to help you bring your product to the marketplace. That's right, I said "product"; your sweet little song, your eccentric screenplay, your new app or tech toy is, at this point, a product. You're trying to sell it and make money! Grow up!

Some creatives are really good at this part of the process. It's almost shocking to watch such a person shift hats and become a super salesperson. Some songwriters I know are amazing at networking, pitching, and getting their songs "placed" (recorded) with other singers.

There's probably another category of creatives we should mention: those who are so sales- and marketing-oriented that when they start to create, it's already intended for consumption. This approach would align with what we called a *market-driven offering.* "Pure" creatives might look down on such a commercial approach, but once our livelihood is mixed in, we've already more or less left the realm of "pure" creativity. Our heaven will always have some amount of earth dangling from it.

So let's go to your workbook.

📖 30. The Creative Timeline

1. Describe a moment of inception for you, a moment when a creative idea was hatched. What did it feel like? Did you feel inspired? Excited? Exhilarated? Scared?

2. Now talk about the process of working with that idea to develop it: sticking with it, hanging out with it, struggling with it. How did that feel? Can you talk about and compare these feelings?

3. How about finishing a creative project? Again, what feelings accompanied this moment? Relief? Release? Anxiety? Vulnerability?

4. Now talk about a creative project that had no commercial aspect to it, maybe such as planning a surprise thirtieth birthday party for your sister or best friend. Or cooking a great dinner for your family. Or that new paddleless canoe you have invented. What kind of feelings are associated with that kind of creativity?

5. And finally, if appropriate for you, talk about bringing a completed creative project to the marketplace. How did this final stage affect the whole feeling of creating something in the first place? Did you feel expansive and inspired about the prospect of reaching a wider audience? Did you feel cheapened and depressed? Did you feel anxious about facing the competition and a fear of failure? Can you recognize any possible fear of success? ✎

29 Leave Some Space

Form and Emptiness

Nothing exists except atoms and empty space;
everything else is opinion.
                                        —DEMOCRITUS

WE Buddhists talk a lot about *sunyata*, or emptiness. Others might take this to mean that Buddhism is negative or even nihilistic, but that's not actually the case.

Emptiness is just a word used to describe a certain aspect of our reality. When we look at a cloud, for example, we could easily come to the conclusion that the cloud has solid form, that an airplane would bounce off it. To an untrained mind, a cloud appears to have solid form. That's how it appears. But if we look at the cloud over time, if we really study the cloud, we discover its characteristics:

1. It's always changing shape. The form the cloud appears to have is temporary and continuously morphing. At first it looks like a rabbit, then it looks like a hat, then it looks like a blob. It's continuously changing shape.
2. It exists in relationship to the other clouds around it, to the sky, to the lake below it and its reflection in that lake, to the mountains it wraps its form around and sometimes even merges with. The cloud doesn't exist independently. It exists interdependently.
3. It's made up of smaller and smaller components. There's no

singular entity that we can call the cloud—a few puffs here and there, a darker base, a wisp of smoke . . . oops, now it has merged with another "cloud"; two "clouds" are now one.

A cloud is impermanent, interdependent, and multifaceted. Even though it may appear otherwise, essentially it lacks (is empty of) permanent existence, independent existence, singular existence.

In the same way, all external phenomena are empty. We can apply the same process to understand the difference between the appearance and essential nature of trees, rocks, buildings, rivers, mountains, planets, stars, the universe, the multiverse, etc., etc.

In the same way, our body, our thoughts and emotions, our speech, our gestures, our attitudes, our insights, our likes, our dislikes, our indifferences, our relationships, our lives, our reincarnations, our "souls," our narratives, our "selves," others, our mothers, our lovers, our successes, our failures, our mistakes, our insights—all are empty of permanent, independent, and singular existence.

When we really see firsthand that the way all these things appear isn't necessarily how they are, it's kind of mind-blowing. The rug is suddenly pulled out from under our habitual and conventional perceptions of what we take to be solid and "real." Sometimes there are words for this kind of seeing: *satori*, for example, in the Zen tradition.

CTR used to describe enlightenment as ego's final disappointment—we keep trying, unsuccessfully, to shore up our solid self—but there might also be some kind of relief. In a way, it's like waking up from a dream. When we wake up from a dream, it doesn't really matter if it was a good dream or a bad dream; now we're awake.

Mindfulness Meditation II

Let's go back to our basic mindfulness practice for a few minutes. But this session, every time you notice that you're thinking, say "thinking" to yourself. As you come back to your breath and the feeling of being present, say to yourself, with a light touch and a little irony, "now I am awake"—and let it go. Just be with your breath for a while and then, again, when you drift off into the daydream of thoughts, notice and repeat this exercise. Don't try to achieve any particular state of mind and don't try to cling to the feeling of being awake. Notice, touch in, acknowledge, and let go.

There's another element to relating to emptiness. When we see and feel the empty quality in things, we begin to notice that there's space around and inside of things we think of as heavy and solid. That boulder has space around it, even inside it, if we can see it clearly. Our thoughts have space around them and even inside them.

The relationship between form and emptiness is at the center of one of the most universally chanted Buddhist teachings: the *Heart Sutra*. This teaching is the cornerstone of Mahayana Buddhism and is chanted by Buddhists around the world. It's like the "Amazing Grace" of the Buddhist world. It's a tune almost everybody knows and has a version of—different translations, different languages, different melody maybe, but there it is—it's what we call a classic in the music biz.

I think it's fair to say that Zen Buddhism (Chan in China) has an important relationship to the notion of emptiness. In a way, the Zen Buddhism tradition conjoins it to the idea of appreciating the spacious quality of existence. There's room; there's space; you don't have to fill every corner, fill in every detail; you can create and then leave some space.

In Japan they even have a word for this kind of open space. It's called *ma*. I'm not sure there's as good a word in English because in the West, this kind of space tends to get tagged with a negative connotation: a feeling of something missing, something left out; we could be more busy, more active, more proactive—fill it in! But in Japanese culture, this notion of ma is thoroughly ensconced. It's an important element of art and culture such as *noh* theater, *ikebana* (flower arranging), *chado* (tea ceremony), calligraphy, haiku, and especially the practice of formal meditation such as Zen.

This idea is deeply embedded in Japanese culture, but these days it's kind of taking a beating. The notions of productivity, efficiency, and precision—also part of the zeitgeist—have become dominant. Ma, once a precious and singular aspect of life, has become somewhat sidelined in the modern ethos, but it's still there lurking, and it might be a good time for us to bring it off the bench and put it back into the game—both in the East and in the West.

Let's make it a slogan:

Leave some space.

What we're saying here is that, in your creative project, don't cross every *t* and dot every *i*. Leave some room for your audience's imagination (your customer, if you've gone pro). Leave some room for your story to unfold; leave some space between the notes if you're a musician, etc., etc., etc.

In the Buddhist way of thinking, creativity itself arises from space and dissolves back into it. Inhale, exhale: everything in life has those two elements.

Ma

Take your meditation seat again and bring your attention to your breath. Focus in for a few moments as before, notice thoughts arise, label them "thinking," and bring your attention back to your breath.

With eyes open and looking straight ahead, again with a light, diffused visual field, open but unfocused, now try to just relax your effort and agenda, and let the labeling technique fall away. Just rest in the open space of awareness. Relax your agenda and just be present.

After a few moments you can come back to the more meticulous technique you started with. Notice the contrast between these two methods. One emphasizes precision, the other letting go. One is about form and the other is about ma.

Sometimes when we're giving ourselves or others meditation instruction, we could simply say, "More precise," or we could say, "More ma." Eventually we can strike a balance.

I think that's enough said about that. Better to not say too much about emptiness. Let's float on over to your workbook.

31. Emptiness

1. Rest your mind for a few moments. Now write a poem, right now, four lines maximum. First thought, best thought. Then rest your mind for a few more moments. Now read your poem back out loud, to no one in particular. Rest again.

2. How do you relate to the concept of emptiness, space, or ma

in your creative work? Does it already play a role? Do you tend to fill in all the space compulsively?

3. Are you comfortable just resting your mind in a wakeful way? Do you want to have more of a project with your meditation practice? Are you trying to get to some particular state of consciousness that you prefer to this ordinary moment of awareness? Are you "tripping"? ✎

30 Master Your Craft
Patience, Exertion, and Discipline

Excellence is inconveniently difficult.
—WILLIAM H. GASS, *A Temple of Texts*

O F COURSE, everybody knows the famous joke about the violinist who stops a NYC citizen to ask for directions: "Do you know how to get to Carnegie Hall?" The answer? "Practice!"

My perception, as I mentor young entrepreneurs and creatives, is that 70 to 80 percent of the obstacles they face are because they don't yet know what they're doing. They haven't mastered all the elements of their enterprise; they haven't yet mastered the tools of their trade.

When we're not sufficiently trained, we can spend too much time going around in circles, recreating the wheel, recreating all kinds of wheels. For example, these days I spend an inordinate amount of time with logons, passwords, software commands, etc. When I see a millennial friend whipping through their iPhone, I sometimes feel a little bit stupid, but more importantly I feel undertrained in that particular skill set.

For me, it's usually more cost effective to have an assistant manage my social media accounts, for example, than to fully engage in further training in the latest apps and updates. My time is better used engaging in creative projects such as this book or my musical. Maybe that's an excuse . . . but so be it. Sometimes we lean into parts of our world that we enjoy and lean away from those things that we experience as unappealing or stress-inducing. This is OK, as long as we have a system in place to cover the things we shrink from, so they don't hang around and undermine our efforts.

It's critically important, though, that we master the skills that have direct impact on our actual job description. For example, let's say you want to earn a living as a guitar player for hire, available for live performances or recording sessions. In this case, it's *up to you* to master *all* the skills you may be required to have: reading music fluidly, being able to play in a wide variety of styles, having your gear—your instruments, f/x pedals, and amps—in top shape and sounding impeccable. Buzzes, hums, out-of-tune notes, and lapses of concentration won't be appreciated or tolerated.

If you're a salesperson, you have to know everything about sales, including how to create a funnel of potential buyers, move clients through that funnel, and—super importantly—actually close! Salespeople live or die by how productive they are. The measurement is entirely tangible; there's no touchy-feely part of that process. Your work will be assessed by your numbers, period.

However, if you're a marketing person, you're responsible for promoting your brand and merchandise in a more general way. Are people aware of your company and its product? Have you reached the designated target beyond general awareness and into the specific niche for which your product is targeted? Do you understand the role of print and media advertising, PR, and social media?

Mastering your craft will take patience, exertion, and discipline. In general, there are no shortcuts or easy roads for this kind of cultivation. For example, there's no such thing as a great musician who hasn't practiced, at some point in their life, if not throughout their life, for three to five hours a day or more.

I've had the pleasure of working with some of the greatest musicians in the world. It's always startling to see (and hear) the quality of music they're able to produce and generate consistently.

One in particular was Ustad Sultan Khan, one of the great masters of the sarangi, a classical Indian instrument that's a bit like a violin in that there are no frets and the strings are played with a bow. Like many other classical Indian instruments, it has a very vocal sound. Many great musicians recognize that the voice is really the primary and ultimate musical instrument, and some of them can create the illusion that their instrument is singing. Sultan Khan sang through his sarangi. The sound he made was astonishingly penetrating. It went right to the heart.

My record label, 5 Points Records, recorded an album of original music with Khan-sahib. I got to play guitar on the recordings, which was especially thrilling. The music was already a hybrid of East and West, but then we went further and had some highly regarded remixers work with the tracks to make them utterly contemporary and club-worthy for electronica and dance environments.

If you want to check it out the album, it's called *Rare Elements*. It's cool and fun, but I would also recommend you check out some of Sultan Khan's straight-up classical recordings to get the full dose of what we're talking about here. This link will take you to both: davidnichtern.com/khan

We worked on this project for several weeks, so we had lots of time to hang out, grab some great Indian food on Lexington Avenue in Manhattan, and compare notes about various adventures. I was very curious about the kind of training one received as an Indian classical musician. As you can well imagine, they take their training very seriously indeed. Khan-sahib told me about a very special practice situation that a musician of his caliber might be asked to undertake. It involved going into a solitary retreat for something like seven weeks.

In this particular music retreat, the musicians are asked to practice ten to twelve hours a day or more, every day. At one point, Sultan

Khan was practicing so violently that he said the blood was just flying off his fingers and splattering abstract patterns on the wall. This intensive work develops the musicians' technique beyond any kind of limitation; the artists push themselves to the very edge of their capacity and even to the edge of their sanity. Khan-sahib said that when you come out of that retreat, you're either a great master or you never want to touch your instrument again.

In his case, neither of those results happened because he basically started to go nuts and had to bail after five weeks or so. He didn't complete the retreat. In his case you would have never known it. He sounded as if he had done ten such retreats. His playing was flawless and his "feel" and passion were unbelievable.

Of course, intensive retreat is also a part of the Buddhist tradition. My teacher's teacher, Dilgo Khyentse Rinpoche, spent fifteen years in a cave practicing meditation. I often ask my one-hundred-hour mindfulness teacher trainees how many of them would continue to be involved if a fifteen-year retreat was added to the one-hundred-hour requirement!

Long story short, digging in deep in order to perfect our craft is strongly recommended if we want to achieve a high level of success in our creativity and livelihood. There's really no substitute for good old-fashioned patience, exertion, and discipline.

Let's go to your workbook.

32. Mastering Your Craft

1. What are the primary skill sets you use in your creative and business life?
2. How would you assess your level of competency in those skills?
3. In what areas do you think you need to increase your capac-

ity? Business planning? Administration? Content development? Sales? Marketing?

4. How do you propose to get the additional training/mentoring you need to achieve optimal results?

31 Know When to Stop Polishing a Turd

More Letting Go

Never love something so much that you can't let go of it.
And you have to reinvent.

—Ginni Rometty, CEO of IBM

I PRODUCED, composed, and cocomposed the score for the ABC daytime classic *One Life to Live* (*OLTL*) for almost twenty years, and halfway through I also started creating music for CBS's *As the World Turns*. I won four Emmys during that time for these projects.

The person who originally hired me for the *OLTL* job was the highly regarded producer (of *Dirty Dancing* fame) Linda Gottlieb. She was a high-powered New Yorker, with lots of drive and energy. She was a tough businessperson, but she knew exactly what she wanted, so I found her relatively easy to work for. We just had to work hard—but not in the dark.

Linda loved music and was very actively involved in helping shape the musical content and style. She also gave extremely direct feedback. She had no problem at all giving direction and offering straightforward responses to the music we delivered.

And here is where we get to the title of this chapter. If my team and I had come up with a particular theme or cue and were trying to refine it to make it more palatable, better constructed, or more finely crafted, sometimes she would just say, "Stop polishing a turd."

There have been many times since then, when I'm producing

music or working with an artist on my record labels, that I've borrowed and payed forward this exact verbiage. Other expressions include "pouring good sauce on bad meat" or "throwing good money after bad." Lately I've occasionally recommended to someone I'm mentoring to "stop feeding a dead pet." All these phrases convey a similar meaning, but none are as graphic, vivid, and immediately satisfying as Linda's choice phrase.

It can be so valuable to deeply understand the implications of this colorful expression. How many times have we gone down a creative road, a direction in life, a business deal, a particular spiritual approach even, only to find that the fundamental concept wasn't worth the energy and effort we were putting into it?

When we first start something—a relationship, business, song, new product or offering, website, marketing campaign—there's often a kind of excitement, a fresh energy, even a kind of romantic glaze. Inception is a big-bang kind of moment, fresh snow, a sunrise full of possibilities and anticipation. I've never started a new song without feeling, "Wow, this is cool; I really have something here." First-thought energy is powerful, provocative, and inspiring.

When that moment passes, however, we're left with several alternatives:

1. Dig in and work hard to bring our project along toward manifestation (as discussed previously herein). Begin to polish that raw diamond.
2. Bookmark it for when we have more time and can revisit and develop the idea.
3. Take a good, hard second look, anywhere along the road, and abandon ship when we realize that we're not polishing a diamond; we're polishing a turd.

What makes our project a turd rather than a diamond? Well, sometimes it can be difficult to say. But however we get there, we come to realize that somehow the project we're working on isn't that compelling; it's not that interesting, relevant, artful, or well constructed; perhaps it's redundant, maybe a little flat and a little dull. Maybe we come to see this ourselves, maybe we get feedback from trusted friends and advisers, maybe nobody else is interested in hearing it, seeing it, buying it, or even renting it.

I heard a statistic the other day that 90 percent of all entrepreneurs firmly believe they're holding a winning hand with their offering, even though only 10 to 20 percent of them will have any version of success at all.

To be clear, we have to distinguish between a turd and a unique-but-perhaps-difficult-to-recognize gemstone. In the latter case, we can stick to our guns and we may end up with one of those exquisite oddities: a groundbreaking, out-of-the-box, trendsetting, fabulous new offering.

The point here is that we can't just *always* fall in love with our own creation. And sometimes, when we finally wake up and smell the coffee, or the whatever, we have to let it go and start fresh.

OK, let's go to your workbook.

 ## 33. Polishing Turds

1. With a yes or no answer, please just say whether you understand this vital creative concept: "Don't polish a turd."
2. Can you think of a situation in which you found yourself polishing a turd? Tell your story. Make us laugh, make us cry.
3. In full disclosure, is it possible that a project you're working on *right now* falls into this category? That perhaps, as Kevin O'Leary on *Shark Tank* loves to say, "should be taken out behind the barn and shot"?

4. Can you identify the part of yourself that has difficulty recognizing this kind of project and becomes attached to it against all common sense? Is it denial? Nostalgia? Laziness? Stubbornness? Pride? What were you thinking? ☺ ✎

Epilogue: It's Not Over Until It's Over . . . Now It's Over

THESE DAYS, whenever I start any kind of episode, trip, retreat, or adventure, I visualize it being over right from the start. (This, by the way, at the tender age of seventy, includes this particular lifetime.) In the Zen tradition, they look at a cup and say, "It's already broken." I think the meaning is clear.

I contemplate cessation every single day and in a variety of ways. You might think that this nod to impermanence and cessation is nihilistic and depressing, and at its worst you would be right, but there's another aspect that's liberating and expansive: You can think of your life and your career as a beautiful flower arrangement. It's fragile, and ultimately doomed, but it's also beautiful, and you can put your best heart and mind into it—all the way.

In this book, I've tried to share a big piece of my life experience with all of you. I like giving advice; it's kind of in my DNA. Obviously sometimes people don't want my advice; Master Hon once told me, "Eat your own noodles." For some strange reason, most of the people in my immediate family—including my son, my sister, and my beloved Monika—at times don't seek out (or even put up with) the extensive nudging for which I now often receive the medium bucks from total strangers.

Sometimes each of us may just be looking for approval, confirmation, or just some space and respect, and feel that we need those things more than we need penetrating insight or suggestions.

Everybody has felt that way, including me. As Uncle Irv used to say, "You can't tell anybody something unless they *have a place to put it.*"

There's an art to giving feedback, advice, and constructive criticism. Of course, we can start with something positive, both to create some ground for the conversation and also to relax the recipient before we slide the blade between their ribs (just kidding!). My dentist vigorously massages my gums before injecting me with Novocain and I can hardly feel it when he slips in the needle. Seriously.

But really seriously, we should be mindful when giving feedback and advice. Even if the advice is legitimately helpful, if there's too much of our own agenda and projections in the mix, we won't be helping somebody; we'll be annoying them.

The beauty of a book like this, and my hope for you the reader, is that you can just take the best and leave the rest. Perhaps your own workbook and process of discovery will dwarf any little tidbits offered here.

But if there's value for you, please know that I'm happy about that. I genuinely hope that this offering helps you clarify your vision and manifest it for the benefit of yourself and all beings. As I wrote in one of my own damn songs, "Leaves Inside a Storm":

> Please take a piece as you leave me,
> And please feel free to leave a piece behind.
> Travel life's railway to heaven,
> We'll meet at the end of the line.

So thank you for sharing this little journey with me. You can put the book down now and move on. Come back again anytime for a visit.

I'll close by repeating the words of my teacher Chögyam Trungpa Rinpoche: "Your guess is as good as mine. Good luck!"

And now, your final trip to your workbook.

 34. And in the End

1. Feel free to write whatever you wish in conclusion. Perhaps you can have a fresh look at your first entry and have a second pass at it. *How're you doin'?* ✎

Acknowledgments
and Special Thanks

Dan, Kestrel, Laura, and Alexandra at Wisdom, Master Sat Hon, Stephanie Tade, Seth Freedman, Amy Dewhurst, Rebecca D'Onofrio, Suketaka Kawazu, Nicky, Ethan, and Monika—with love and appreciation.

Appendix 1:
Meditation Instructions

Mindfulness Meditation

View

Shamatha, meaning "calm abiding" in Sanskrit, is the foundation of the practice that's referred to as "mindfulness." Mindfulness meditation can be defined as learning to bring our attention to the present moment, by focusing on our breath, and simply seeing what arises without bias or judgment. When our attention wanders, and we notice, we simply return our attention to our breath. Mindfulness is simple and straightforward. The benefit of this practice is that we become more synchronized in body and mind, and we begin to relate to our world in a less distracted and more wakeful way. By returning our attention to the present, we can cut through the accumulation of stress and anxiety and develop clarity, strength, and stability in our everyday lives.

Instructions

1. Take Your Seat

Start by taking your meditation seat, usually a solid cross-legged sitting position on a cushion on the floor. You'll want to get into a comfortable posture with a good firm connection between your butt and the cushion—you should feel grounded and stable. Then you can just rest your hands on your thighs or your knees, depending on how long your arms are.

Your torso, head, and shoulders should be upright but relaxed. Then just gently tuck your chin in a little bit. The posture should feel dignified and uplifted but not stiff or tense: upright but not uptight.

If you have trouble sitting cross-legged for whatever reason, you can take a kneeling posture with a cushion for support or sit upright on a chair. Sitting on a chair is completely fine. The main point is that you should use whatever support you need (cushions, etc.) to be comfortable, but in any of these positions your back should be as upright as possible and not supported by the wall or the back of the chair if possible." Not too tight and not too loose" is a good guideline all the way through.

There's a feeling of containment, of taking your seat and reducing your sphere of activity. Then, make sure your jaw is relaxed, your mouth either lightly closed or slightly open. Your eyes should be open with a soft downward gaze, maybe four to six feet on the floor in front of you. You're not shutting down awareness of the space around you, but you can relax your focus somewhat.

During longer periods of sitting, if you need to move to restore your circulation, or when you have real discomfort, you can just bring your legs up in front of your chest and continue your practice. Then just resettle yourself and take a fresh start.

2. Place Your Attention on Your Breath

Having settled your body in this way, you begin to pay attention to your breathing—in and out. In this case it's natural breathing—not any particular breathing technique, just ordinary breathing. Your awareness becomes connected to your breath. Here, again, use a light touch rather than becoming too intense and hyperfocused— just a nice relaxed attentiveness to your breath going in and out of your body. You can focus on the feeling of your breath at the tip of your nose or simply experience the full cycle of breath throughout your body.

When you notice that your awareness is elsewhere—maybe you're thinking of your relationship, your workweek coming up, or a big bowl of chocolate ice cream—just bring your attention back to your breathing, without any kind of judgment, commentary, or evaluation. Just bring it back.

3. Label Thoughts as Thinking

When you notice that you're lost in thoughts, you can just say to yourself, "thinking." Just label it with that one word, *thinking*, and then bring your attention back once again to your breath. You're not trying to struggle against your mind. Your thoughts are not the enemy. You're not repressing your thoughts and neither are you following them. You're simply letting them be as they are, noticing them, and then returning your attention to your breath.

That's a basic introduction to the technique of mindfulness meditation—how to go about it. It's OK to start modestly at first, maybe sitting once every other day for ten or fifteen minutes or so. From there you can build up to a daily sitting practice of however long feels right for you. A daily practice of even twenty minutes can substantially shift the quality of your life. Once you get underway, working with a teacher can be very helpful. Meditating in a group setting can also be beneficial and can give you context, structure, and support for your practice.

WALKING MEDITATION

View

Walking meditation is a variation on mindfulness practice. It gives us a chance to refresh our body during longer practice sessions, and it also serves as a bridge to practicing mindfulness in everyday life and activity.

Instructions

In walking meditation you take a good upright standing posture. Use a hand mudra, or gesture; make your left hand into a fist (thumb inside) and place it just below your navel. Wrap your right hand around the left and place your right thumb in the crevice between your left thumb and index finger.

Mindful attention is transferred from the breath to the feeling of the feet and legs moving through space, connecting with the ground and releasing. Use a light touch to your awareness of movement. You don't need to label thoughts as "thinking." Simply feel the movement of your legs and feet and notice what arises without judgment or evaluation. When you notice that your attention has wandered, simply bring it back.

The pace is slower than normal but not exaggeratedly slow. If practicing in a group, the group should move in a clockwise motion and keep equal spacing between each person as much as possible.

Awareness Meditation

View

In mindfulness we begin our practice by focusing our attention on one particular object—most commonly the feeling of the breath going in and out of our body. As thoughts, feelings, sensations, and perceptions arise, we notice them without judgment or evaluation, and simply bring our attention back to our breath or the object of our concentration. In awareness practice, however, we begin to tune in to the greater environment in which our focused attention is taking place.

An analogy to help us understand the relationship between mindfulness and awareness is playing basketball: The mindfulness aspect of playing basketball is our ability to focus on the basketball—we're very tuned in to the location of the ball and not losing our relationship with it. In basketball, the coach might say, "Keep your eye on the ball"; here we say, "Place your attention on your breath." The awareness aspect is expanding your field of attention outward: into the court, the position of our teammates as well as our opponents, the time left on the clock, even our own thoughts and feelings as we play, and so on.

Another analogy is driving: The mindfulness aspect is keeping our hands on the steering wheel and our eyes on the road. The awareness aspect is the full expanse of the environment, the position of the other vehicles, the exit signs, and so on. Mindfulness and awareness work together to help us synchronize our mind and body in the present moment with our outer environment and inner experience.

With awareness practice we shift our attention from being focused primarily on just our breathing (as with mindfulness practice) toward the situation as a whole, which includes our breathing, sense perceptions, bodily sensations, thoughts, and emotions. There's a sense of lightening our effort as we simply notice what arises within the field of our full range of experience. Mindfulness brings our attention back and gives us focus; awareness illuminates the entire situation.

Instructions

Take a comfortable seat in a quiet place. Begin with a few moments of mindfulness practice. When you feel ready, expand your awareness by tuning in to the whole environment. Place approximately (remember the light touch here!) 25 percent of your attention on your breathing, about 25 percent on noticing the texture of thoughts and feelings that arise, about 25 percent on physical sensations and sense perceptions, and leave the remaining 25 percent open.

Start by moving through the sense fields as the object of your attention. For instance:

- **Sound**: Simply close your eyes and listen to the environment. Your experience of hearing becomes the focal point of your meditation. When your mind wanders, simply come back to whatever you're hearing in the moment.
- **Sight**: Starting with your head and eyes all the way to the left, scan slowly from left to right, taking around three to four minutes to complete the scan. Just see whatever is in front of you as fully and vividly as you can without attempting to characterize or evaluate what you see. When your mind wanders, simply come back to the experience of your visual field.
- **Taste**: Try a mindful snack—eat one simple food (a raisin, for example) slowly and with full awareness of all sensations. This is the opposite of mindlessly pigging out and is a very informative practice regarding our relationship to food.

If you find yourself spacing out or getting lost, you can always place more of your attention on your breathing and as you feel ready, expand out again. You can end your practice with a few moments of mindfulness practice with a stronger focus on your breath.

CONTEMPLATIVE MEDITATION

View

In contemplative meditation, we use our thinking mind to deepen our understanding of a particular topic or aspect of our experience. This practice helps us ignite our curiosity and cultivate discernment (*prajna*, in Sanskrit), which we can apply in our everyday lives.

In the Buddhist teachings, we're encouraged not to simply take the teacher's word but rather to verify the teachings through the lens of our own experience.

The Three Prajnas:

1. Hearing
   a. Reading a book, listening to a talk, attending a class, etc.

2. Contemplating
   a. Processing the information and moving toward direct, personal understanding
   b. Internalizing and analyzing what we have heard; mixing it with our experience

3. Meditating
   a. Direct understanding
   b. Experiencing the meaning of what we have contemplated

Instructions

Choose a topic for your contemplation. Take a comfortable seat in a quiet place. Begin with a few moments of mindfulness practice. When you feel ready, shift your focus from your breathing to the topic you have chosen for your contemplation. You can repeat a key word or phrase in your mind a few times. You can ask yourself related questions to help deepen your exploration of the topic. You can let ideas and images arise as you contemplate the topic.

Notice what arises for you: thoughts, feelings, sensations. As with mindfulness practice, if your mind wanders away from the contemplation, just notice that and gently bring it back to the topic. Continue to dig deeper and deeper. When you feel you can't go any further with the topic, let all the thoughts, images, questions, etc., drop away and let your mind simply rest with the meaning or the feeling of it.

Five or ten minutes of contemplation can be plenty for starters. You can end your practice with a few moments of mindfulness meditation by bringing your attention to your breathing, noticing when you wander, labeling thoughts as thinking, and bringing your attention back to your breathing. Often there will be a residual feeling or insight that lingers, and that's fine.

LOVING-KINDNESS MEDITATION

View

The practice of cultivating loving-kindness (*maitri* in Sanskrit; *metta* in Pali) is a Buddhist approach toward opening one's heart to others. It's very ancient, very simple, very direct, and very effective. It's a variation of contemplative practice.

To prepare the ground for practicing loving-kindness, it can be helpful to consider the following:

- **Impermanence**: We can contemplate the fact that the way in which we categorize other beings will change over time, sometimes very quickly, sometimes more slowly. Whatever we experience is subject to impermanence.

  For example, an anonymous person we meet in the supermarket can become our lover, and later on can become our husband or wife, and later on become our not-so-welcome (in some cases) ex-wife or ex-husband! We've gone through the three basic responses of ignorance, attachment, and aversion with just one person!

- **Causes and Conditions**: In this practice, we recognize that the way we look at people is very much related to causes and conditions. It's not absolute. If we're having a bad day, it's much easier to get irritated at somebody, maybe even somebody we fundamentally like. If we've had an abusive childhood, we can feel that the whole world is against us and we want to strike back. If it's a beautiful sunny spring day, everybody looks great and we're in love with everything and everyone.

  Causes and conditions set the stage for our attitudes toward the world, and we can and do affect those causes and conditions. It's practical to train our minds further so that we're not governed by our negative habitual patterns.

- **Absolute and Relative Bodhicitta** (awakened heart and

mind): In this practice, we explore our most fundamental nature. What are we like when we're open, clear, and fully present? What is our true nature?

We also explore compassion. Do we really wish others to suffer? Do we really wish to create the causes and conditions for our own suffering? It's possible to cultivate open-hearted and positive wishes for ourselves and others, and this practice will help us achieve that goal.

Instructions

The heart of this practice is generating four positive wishes for all beings:

- May you be safe.
- May you be healthy.
- May you be happy.
- May you be at ease.

We include beings we care for (attachment), those we don't care for (aversion), and those we don't care about (ignorance). We even include ourselves!

Practicing loving-kindness is simple and direct. Just take a comfortable seat in a quiet place and close your eyes. First think of somebody you love. Send them the four wishes. You can either repeat each for a time with that person in mind or just think about how those wishes might manifest and affect that situation. You can be creative about it.

Then move on successively to yourself, a neutral person (somebody you don't know well or don't have strong feelings about), and then finally take the plunge and send the wishes to an "enemy" (somebody you find irritating or annoying is fine). You may even notice that the choice of who the enemy is changes, and that's fine. As mentioned already, yesterday's enemy could be tomorrow's ally.

Also, it's fine just to notice what comes up for you while you're trying to do this practice and simply allow space for that as well.

Naturally, it's easier to generate these positive wishes for our parents (in most cases), our children, our pets, our teachers, or our friends. In these instances, loving-kindness flows unimpeded.

It's challenging to generate that kind of attitude toward people to whom we're indifferent, and it's very challenging indeed to generate it toward people we don't like or even hate. For some of us it can be most challenging to generate this attitude toward ourselves.

At the end, conclude by simply radiating out your loving-kindness—your kind, sweet, loving, open heart—to all beings and send your good wishes to all of them: friends, yourself, neutrals, enemies, humans, animals, ghosts—anybody you can think of. Then simply dissolve the meditation and sit quietly for a moment or two.

Loving-kindness is an ancient practice dating all the way back to the Buddha, and it can be surprisingly powerful.

FREQUENTLY ASKED QUESTIONS FOR MINDFULNESS MEDITATION

• **I'm used to meditating with my eyes closed. Why are you recommending keeping my eyes open with a soft downward gaze?**

In this approach to meditation practice, we're not shutting down our sense perceptions or trying to move into some inner realm or trance state. We're simply being present, paying attention to our breath, and noticing what arises in our mind and sense perceptions. Our awareness is somewhat subdued and we're staying put and being quiet (hence our eyes are open but with a slightly downward gaze), but at the same time we're setting the stage for moving back into our active world without too much contrast, so that we can continue to be awake and mindful as we move through our everyday life.

• **Are sense perceptions thoughts? Emotions? What do I do with sensations, strong sensory perceptions, and emotions? Do I just label them all "thinking"?**

When we notice we're thinking, whether about our perceptions and sensations or our emotions, we can still label those thoughts as "thinking." If there are more direct experiences of sense perceptions or the energetic aspect of our emotions, we can just leave those experiences as they are without further elaboration. We're neither trying to repress or evaluate them.

• **What about physical pain? How do I deal with that? My back/ knees are killing me!**

Above all we should be kind to ourselves. Obviously we need to develop discipline for this or any other practice, but I'm not recommending self-torture and denial here. If the pain becomes intense, we can just shift our posture, take a fresh start, and continue. If we have ongoing pain in our back or legs, for example, we can try a different posture such as kneeling or sitting on a chair. We can also use a variety of support cushions to make the posture more workable. Talk to your meditation teacher for help in this area.

- **Can I meditate leaning back or lying down? Walking? Swimming? Running?**

  Better to sit up unsupported, if possible. That's the most ergonomic posture for supporting this effort to be wakeful and relaxed at the same time. The posture is important. Of course, you can practice mindfulness while engaged in any kind of activity (even late-night snacking), but without the formal sitting practice, many people throughout history have found it to be nearly impossible to cultivate mindfulness in everyday life. Think of the two—stillness and activity—as a happy couple.

- **Sometimes my mind is like a jungle of thoughts that just won't quit. How do I deal with that?**

  You're not alone! That's a big part of why most people meditate. I recommend that you keep your basic discipline of "not too tight and not too loose." Remember to come back to your breath when you can but don't beat yourself up when your mind is particularly active. Take a gentle but firm approach as you would with a rowdy child.

- **When should I meditate? How often? How long? How should I time it?**

  It's best to meditate at a regular time every day, if possible. If not, just do the practice when you can. For beginners, twenty minutes a day can be transformative. If you can only do ten minutes per day for starters, that's way better than nothing. If you miss a day, don't beat yourself up; just come back to it the next day. You can use any of the timer apps that are out there or simply look at your watch or clock periodically—no big deal.

- **Can I journal while meditating?**
  No, but you can journal after if you like. Otherwise you're not meditating, you're journaling!

- **What about listening to music?**
  It's better to leave the space open and clear so you can avoid any kind of distraction, even a pleasant one.

THE DEDICATION OF MERIT

This is a short chant, that you can include (if you wish) at the end of your session, to share the benefits of your practice with others.

May all beings be happy.
May all beings be free from suffering.
May all beings feel joy in the happiness of others.
May all beings remain in equanimity free from attachment,
 aversion, and ignorance.

Appendix 2:
Slogans

With meditation practice there are various benefits, but none of them can be realized if you don't **make the time to actually practice**.

The need to create may be a personal one—but for your creation to serve a market or an audience, you must **be aware of the needs of others**.

If your time and energy are spread too thinly across a variety of (possibly wonderful) offerings, some or all of them may falter.

Good leaders take responsibility. If you find that you're constantly pointing out the shortcomings of others, turn the mirror around so it's facing you.

Take your mind to the gym. Just as you can train your body to develop strength, flexibility, and stamina, you can also train your mind to develop clarity, focus, and stability.

If your mind is a runaway train, your life will be a runaway life.

The first step is to clearly define your offering. It can be a service, a product, or intellectual property. It comes from who you are, what you're good at, and what you create in your life to present to others.

Your offering should be the best it can possibly be. **Refining your offering will require effort and energy.**

In order for your offering to meet the marketplace, you should **know your market**, have some idea of its size, and know how to communicate with the people in that market.

Some offerings come out of your personal creativity. Others are designed to meet a specific market need (such as creating a can opener once cans have hit the market).

Overcome poverty mentality.

Don't forget to feed the cash cow!

Bring awareness to the situation.

To bring awareness to your situation, cultivate the art of attention. Learn how to place, direct, and focus your attention.

Hone your intention.

Respect your mind and your body.

Respect other people's minds and bodies.

Move toward the light and keep going.

Rouse a sense of confidence and uplifted energy.

Leave some space.

Traditional Buddhist Slogans

Not too tight and not too loose.

Of the two witnesses, take the principal one.

Don't bring things to a painful point.

About the Author

 DAVID NICHTERN has had a diverse life and career as a Buddhist teacher, composer, guitarist, producer, and entrepreneur.

BUDDHISM

David is a senior teacher in the lineage of Chögyam Trungpa Rinpoche. This tradition combines a contemporary, secular approach to meditation with the ancient practices and philosophies of Tibetan Buddhism.

David has been codirector of the Karmê Chöling Meditation Center in Vermont and the Dharmadhatu Meditation Center of Los Angeles, and director of Buddhist Practice and Study for OM yoga.

He has been a featured writer and regular contributor to the *Huffington Post*, and he leads meditation workshops and teacher training programs around the world and online. He has several workshops available through creativeLIVE.com.

David's critically acclaimed book, *Awakening from the Daydream: Reimagining the Buddha's Wheel of Life*, was published by Wisdom Publications in October 2016.

MUSIC

Nichtern is also a well-known composer, producer, and guitarist—a four-time Emmy winner and a two-time Grammy nominee. He's the founder of Dharma Moon and 5 Points Records and has worked with Stevie Wonder, Christopher Guest, Jerry Garcia, Lana Del Rey, Maria Muldaur, Paul Simon, Krishna Das, and many others.

He's the composer of the classic song "Midnight at the Oasis" and has scored feature films such as Christopher Guest's *The Big Picture.* He also composed and produced the scores and title songs for ABC's *One Life to Live* and CBS's *As the World Turns* for many years.

Recently he has been producing and touring with Grammy-nominated kirtan artist Krishna Das and is also creating a new musical titled *Tokyo Swing*—a unique blend of jazz and classical Japanese music—inspired by his frequent visits to Japan to teach Buddhism there.

ENTREPRENEUR

From 1980 to 1987 Nichtern was a distributor for and then director of sales for New England Digital, which created the innovative Synclavier Digital Audio System. He was an integral part of a management team that took the company from $200,000 to $25 million dollars in annual sales during that time.

David also has run his own music production company (Nudgie Music LLC) since 1985 and created two boutique record labels: Dharma Moon and 5 Points Records. Dharma Moon primarily focused on world- and New Age–style releases, while 5 Points Records focused on pop and electronica music. Among 5 Points' significant signings was Lana Del Rey in 2007.

MENTORING & CONSULTING

All these strands have come together in a mentoring program in which David works with individual students and supports them in one or more of these aspects of their evolution—whether it be their individual meditation practice, their creative and personal lives, an evolving entrepreneurial venture, or most likely, some combination of the three.

More about all of the above at davidnichtern.com or facebook.com/davidnichtern.

What to Read Next from Wisdom Publications

Awakening from the Daydream
Reimagining the Buddha's Wheel of Life
David Nichtern

"A wonderful extension of the powerful Dharma teachings of Chögyam Trungpa Rinpoche. The transmission of these ancient lineages is intact in David's hands as he continues to update the traditional Buddhist teachings and make them ever more accessible to the contemporary audience."—Ram Dass, author of *Be Here Now*

One City
A Declaration of Interdependence
Ethan Nichtern

"Resonant and refreshing."—*The American Prospect*

The Mindful Writer
Dinty Moore

"Small but powerful—a welcome addition to many writers' desks, and an inspiring and supportive gift."—*ForeWord*

Living Mindfully
At Home, at Work, and in the World
Deborah Schoeberlein David

"Simple, direct, and full of real-world wisdom, Deborah's excellent new book is for everyone interested in bringing mindful awareness into their daily lives."
—Susan Kaiser Greenland, author of *The Mindful Child*

Mindfulness in Plain English
Bhante Gunaratana

"A classic—one of the very best English sources for authoritative explanations of mindfulness."
—Daniel Goleman, author of *Emotional Intelligence*

Wholehearted
Slow Down, Help Out, Wake Up
Koshin Paley Ellison

"Intimacy is based on the willingness to open ourselves to many others, to family, friends, and even strangers, forming genuine and deep bonds based on common humanity. Koshin Paley Ellison's teachings share the way forward into a path of connection, compassion, and intimacy." —His Holiness the Dalai Lama

About Wisdom Publications

Wisdom Publications is the leading publisher of classic and contemporary Buddhist books and practical works on mindfulness. To learn more about us or to explore our other books, please visit our website at wisdompubs.org or contact us at the address below.

Wisdom Publications
199 Elm Street
Somerville, MA 02144 USA

We are a 501(c)(3) organization, and donations in support of our mission are tax deductible.

Wisdom Publications is affiliated with the Foundation for the Preservation of the Mahayana Tradition (FPMT).